The Queen of Sheba

THE QUEEN OF SHEBA

H. ST JOHN PHILBY

QUARTET BOOKS
LONDON MELBOURNE NEW YORK

First published by Quartet Books Limited 1981
A member of the Namara Group
27 Goodge Street, London W1P 1FD

ISBN 0 7043 2246 3

Printed in Great Britain

Contents

Illustrations

Colour

SECTION ONE

SECTION TWO

Black and white

INTRODUCTION

CHAPTER ONE

CHAPTER TWO

Picture number

CHAPTER THREE

Picture number

CHAPTER FOUR

Picture number

CHAPTER FIVE

Picture number

CHAPTER SIX

Picture number

CHAPTER SEVEN

Picture number

CHAPTER EIGHT

Picture number

The publishers wish to thank
Sue Lubbock for her painstaking
picture research and
Dr Arthur Irvine for his invaluable advice.

Chronology

c. 960-930 B.C.	Reign of Solomon
858-824	Shalmaneser III of Assyria. Yâkinu king of the Sea-land
745-728	Tiglath-Pileser III of Assyria; Zabibe and Shamsi queens of the Arabs
721-705	Sargon II of Assyria; Iti'amarą king of Sabâ
705-681	Sennacherib of Assyria; Yati'e, Talhunu, Tabu'a queens of the Arabs; Karibilu king of Sabâ
after 650	Emergence of Sabâ in South Arabia
c. 550	Taimâ and Dedan flourishing
c. 535	Composition of I Kings
521-486	Darius I of Persia
after 500	Earliest South Arabian inscriptions
485-465	Xerxes I of Persia
465-424	Artaxerxes I of Persia
c. 332	Composition of II Chronicles
c. 150	Rise of the Nabataeans
44	Earliest Palmyrene inscription
106 A.D.	Romans annex Nabataea
129	Palmyra is made free city by Hadrian and rises to prosperity
c. 160	'Alhân Nahfân king of Sabâ
c. 220	Ilsharah Yahdib king of Sabâ
241-272	Shâpûr I of Persia
267	Septimius Odainât of Palmyra murdered after defeating Shâpûr I. He is succeeded by Wahballât with Zenobia as regent. She seizes Syria, Egypt and parts of Asia Minor
271	Zenobia proclaims Wahballât Augustus
272	Defeat of Zenobia by Aurelian leads to decline of Palmyra
c. 300	Shamir Yuhar'ish, son of Yasēr Yuhan'im, king of Himyar
310-379	Shâpûr II of Persia
c. 400	Abkarib As'ad king of Himyar
c. 450	Sharhab'il Ya'fur king of Himyar
c. 525	Dhû Nuwâs king of Himyar persecutes Christians in South Arabia, is deposed and commits suicide
c. 530	Abraha becomes king of Himyar. Final collapse of Mârib dam
after 570	Sassanians occupy South Arabia
622	Muhammad migrates from Mecca to Medina. Start of Muslim era

Introduction

Harry St John Philby, author of *The Queen of Sheba* now published posthumously, spent most of his life roaming the Arabian deserts and writing about unknown oases and their ruler, Ibn Saud. Philby had been deputed to join Ibn Saud from the British Indian Political Service in 1917 and by the end of the war was to receive the Companionship of the Indian Empire and be given the Gold Medal of the Royal Geographical Society, London for his industrious recording of local topography while travelling under the protection of Ibn Saud. He had begun his career in India as a member of the civil service in 1908 and how it was that he left that service and devoted himself to live in Arabia can at least in part be owed to the extraordinary character of Ibn Saud.

When Philby joined him in 1917 he, Ibn Saud, was already well launched on his mastering of the vast country of which he was to become King. As an exile in Kuwait, driven out with his father by the pro-Turk Emir of Hail, he had taught himself to understand the ways of the bedouin and while still in his twenties had been able to recapture the family oasis of Riyadh in the first year of the century. Fire-arms were then rather expensive and javelins and swords were still in use. Ibn Saud, immensely tall for an Arabian, about six foot four, and proportionately strong had thus an advantage in battle in frightening his foes; nevertheless he did have many hand to hand fights and was several times wounded. He would tell rare visitors, like Captain Shakespear, the political agent of the British at Kuwait, of those days, of desert lore and the history of his land, showing he had learnt much from his experiences.

A marked characteristic was his inquisitiveness. In it he indulged himself and when sometimes he came upon what seemed beneficial to him he quickly took it up. In the Persian Gulf states the rulers habitually had a secretary, often a Persian by blood, like Mollah Salah of

Kuwait who was succeeded by his son Abdulla. Ibn Saud gradually acquired a number of educated Levantines; Syrians, Lebanese, Palestinians; who according to their training were given suitable posts. A more unusual function was that of news gatherers, whose sources were the media in general; newspapers from abroad, and Arab and English encyclopedias.

1
King Abdul Aziz Ibn Saud

2
The ‘Ajmân bedouin on the march

Later came the radio stations. One matter which Philby was told to investigate quickly and closely was the possible use of *Magorny*. With a rapidly increasing size of territory, the southern province of Asir added in 1920, Hail in the following year, Jauf in 1922, and the Hijaz four years later, it did seem that Marconi, if Ibn Saud understood its capabilities aright, was exactly what was essential to keep the provinces in touch with him and enable him when it was necessary to send off to them one of his small, now armed motorized columns. The fall to him of the Hijaz came just in time for him, when his need for money was becoming pressing. In 1938 the findings of promised oil in Kuwait and Saudi Arabia had put up the future financial standing and credit of both countries very considerably. So the almost complete stoppage of the pilgrimage plus the loss of the import trade from India owing to the diversion of ships by the powers at war in 1939, would have been disastrous for Saudi Arabia had not England, and then the United States of America, seen good reason for supporting Ibn Saud.

3
Jauf oasis, looking north-west from the Qasr al-Mârid, a stone fortress of the second or third century A.D.

4
The interior of the Qasr al-Mârid at Jauf

5
Ibn Saud's standard bearers

6
Some of the Bin Saud sheikhs inspecting the well pit in the garden at Shamsîya

Long before, in 1912, he had begun a series of agricultural experiments, digging wells, issuing seed and implements and alloting of men with agricultural knowledge to clusters of bedouin united by devotion to the puritanism revered in the past in the Saudi family and their followers. If anything the project was finally too successful in the degree of puritanism it created. Twenty years later Ibn Saud found the movement was out of hand and was obliged to reorganize it.

Such a brief sketch is hardly fair to so great a man, and a truly great man he most certainly was. One of his attributes was his care in selecting friends and subordinates and his loyalty to them however they turned out. He remained considerate to Philby who in later years possibly thought of himself as a kind of Boswellian recorder of the king he admired, though he recorded more of himself than might be expected if only that and geography had been his main reasons for writing.

The fairies, who some pretend meet daily to distribute gifts to the newly born, were certainly distracted when it came to Philby's turn. Qualities generally held to be desirable, great academic ability for one, were unrelieved by touches of others that go to make a tolerable whole. A superfluous gift he credited to himself was ability to prophesy. He even thought he had transmitted it to Kim, saying in his autobiographical book* that he, his son, had shown prophetic insight worthy of his parentage in predicting the result of the civil war in Spain.

7
A street in Jedda

**Arabian Days*, H. St J. Philby, Hale 1948 p. 306.

Supernatural agencies, he believed, were at work influencing his own life. His birth, as he described it, was exactly nine months after the murder in Arabia of the French explorer Charles Huber. 'It is surely no mere coincidence that I was born then, to assume the mantle in due course, of the great Frenchman whose spirit sought the hospitality of my mother's womb, to be re-fashioned therein through a period of stress and storm unequalled in the Victorian Age.'

On his fiftieth birthday, spent in Jedda, the agencies were again at work for him. The elements blew and blustered unceasingly, he records, and then set fire to the reed-hutted suburb of Jedda, whence the Nigerian inhabitants fled helter-skelter in noisy terror.

He made his origin mysterious by relating that while still a baby, born in Ceylon, his parents left him behind by mistake when setting out on a journey, improbable as that must seem. Servants sent back to look for him found that a gipsy woman was taking care of him, but had divided 'his sumptuous clothes' and dressed her own baby in half of them. 'She stoutly declared that having distributed the clothing of the one among the two in proportions which seemed to her more just than those ordained by higher powers, she ceased to be able to distinguish her own babe from my Mother's . . . and no-one to this day knows whether it was myself or the gipsy's child that might have been the rightful heir to the greater part of Leadenhall Street if my great-grandfather had continued poultering . . .'

Since Philby senior was fair in complexion with China blue eyes and stoutly built, anyone more unlike the child of a lithe and dark Sinhalese gipsy it is hard to imagine.

8
Philby with his wife to be, Dora Johnston, in the Punjab in 1910

Next he tells us that a meteorite fell in Ceylon, but that his nurse did not realize the significance of an occurrence that presaged the discovery by him of the great meteorite at Wabar in the depths of the Empty Quarter of Arabia.

The date of his birth, he adds, was a Good Friday, 'the exact anniversary of the Crucifixion, the 3rd. April, 1885.'

At the age of six he returned with his parents from Ceylon, where they were obliged to give up their plantation, to England. At a preparatory boarding school he showed quite unusual talent, and was able to enter Westminster with a scholarship, later becoming Head Boy. From Westminster he went to Cambridge, entering Trinity College and passing the difficult exam into the Indian Civil Service, which he joined in 1908.

In India he met his wife to be, Dora Johnston, daughter of an Executive Engineer in the Rawal Pindi Public Works Department, his best man at the marriage being one, Bernard Montgomery, a lieutenant in the Warwickshire Regiment.

Philby was soon in trouble in India. He was reprimanded for lack of tact and for indiscretion in the case of an assistant surgeon and a sweeper arrested by his order over an alleged false postmortem. The press raised 'an indignant howl' because the two men, the respectable doctor and the sweeper, were chained together by the police on their way to the place of trial. Next he was in trouble for snatching an umbrella out of the hands of a schoolmaster and boxing his ears in front of the boys, the master having passed him without lowering his umbrella, then considered disrespectful. The man and the press made the most of it, and the Government's attention being drawn, Philby was again reprimanded, so losing his chances of acting as a Deputy Commissioner in the hot weather, with all that meant in the way of extra pay. Such acting rank brought about five hundred pounds, and was relied upon by juniors to eke out living expenses, a prize much needed by married ones. As a result he took to studying languages and passing exams in them, which he did brilliantly, one after the other, including Persian and Arabic with Degrees of Honour and large rewards in each case.

Not many officials of the Indian Civil Service spoke Arabic when an Indian expeditionary force began to land in Mesopotamia in October 1914 and Philby was soon sent to join the Chief Political Officer, Sir Percy Cox.

Neither Philby nor his wife having any worthwhile private income or social pull in the peacetime Indian set, he had not felt at home there, and he seemed to go out of his way to rub it in that he was a socialist,

9
Sir Percy Cox

and so tease starchier ladies inclined to snub him. In the hurly-burly, his energies should have been fully taken up and his tendency to take umbrage be without cause.

As assistant to Cox in Baghdad all seemed to be going well for him until Arnold Wilson, who had been in political charge at Basra, came to Baghdad. Wilson was clever and ambitious, and, having served with Cox, hoped to become Deputy Civil Commissioner. He and Philby were at loggerheads without delay. Cox, according to Philby, was indefatigably industrious though having as a 'principal weakness, a tendency to be influenced by dominant personalities', clearly a reference to Wilson, later Sir Arnold Wilson, a British M.P., to be killed as a rear-gunner, R.A.F., and to Gertrude Bell, a linguist, writer and traveller of unequalled experience and erudition about the peoples in the area, who was acting as Oriental Secretary and go-between for the tribes to Cox.

10
Gertrude Bell

Cox, who may have concealed it, was doubtless more in favour of having Wilson with him than Philby. Philby's own version is that he made the condition of giving way, his appointment instead as head of mission to Ibn Saud in central Arabia. The fact that Colonel Hamilton, a former political agent at Kuwait and an Arabist, was already in Riyadh did not seem to disturb either Cox or Philby. The Colonel received no warning of his relief other than the letter from Cox telling him of it, which was handed to him by Philby on his arrival. Hamilton, who afterwards succeeded as Lord Belhaven, is said to have been so taken aback and hurt by this that he had Cox's letter framed and hung in a prominent position in the hall of his place in Scotland for all his visitors to notice. Philby says hardly anything about him, except that he was to the manner born, an Arab in appearance and horsemanship. The reason for his relief was the intrigue in Baghdad. Hamilton had been sent to Ibn Saud following the death of his predecessor in battle while fighting for Ibn Saud against a pro-Turk rival. The main objects of the mission were to pass on to Ibn Saud a subsidy in gold paid by the British Government and concert with him military measures, and both Philby's predecessors were military men.

11
The deck of a pilgrim steamer at Jedda

After the war Philby returned to Baghdad, but not for long. He made no secret of being in favour of a republic there rather than monarchy and was shortly sent to the Emir Abdulla in Trans Jordan, taking over from T. E. Lawrence. He was by now firmly against the policy of the British Government, that of T. E. Lawrence and Gertrude Bell, one of support for the Hashimites, the ruling family of Mecca which had encouraged the revolt in the desert.

Events were to prove Philby right in seeing Ibn Saud as the strong man of the future in Arabia, but he was tactless, and seemed to enjoy being alone versus the rest, a position he was inclined to put himself into more often than not. After a dispute with the High Commissioner in Palestine, Samuel, largely over his own role and the degree of independence he and Trans Jordan were to enjoy, he retired, making his way to Ibn Saud in private capacity and later engaging in business enterprises based on Jedda.

Jedda is one of the hottest places on earth, a port on the steamy, almost landlocked, Red Sea. It was there that the small Christian colony, of Consuls and traders, was confined, and Philby was fortunate to obtain permission to travel inland. Of these journeys he wrote fully, and tediously except for Arabists thirsty for knowledge about the unknown interior.

12
Pilgrims embarking at Jedda

During his many years based in Jedda he had much the same effect on all members of the often changing European Colony, and on Arabs too. They admired his abilities, his knowledge of Arabic and the country, his application to writing – he published in all some fifteen works, totalling about nine hundred thousand or more words – and to whatever was relevant to it, cartography, pre-Islamic archaeology, Arabian ornithology, and the pursuit of his interest in astronomy. But in the end nearly all of them at least temporarily, including Ibn Saud himself, fell out with him.

Philby blamed Ibn Saud for delay in promoting a journey he wished to make through the Empty Quarter of the south, so that he missed the renown of being the very first European ever to make a crossing of the great sands; a bitter blow to him. A European who knew him well, recalling his kindness and generosity to her, also remembers his 'explosions of anger and outbursts of tears', at this time. Another tiff was owed to his making to Ibn Saud a forecast of when the new moon at the beginning of the fasting month of Ramadhan would be seen by man. Ibn Saud, believing that this was something known to God alone, was shocked, as Philby must have known would be the case. Later he was beside himself over the extravagance of Ibn Saud's son and successor, King Saud. He attacked the King in the international

13
Philby's journey into the Empty Quarter, 1932

press about his administration, which did indeed have deplorable faults. As often, Philby was right, which did not prevent King Saud from exiling him from the Kingdom for a year or so.

Philby made a practice of concealing from Europeans the time of his departures on journeys, to the point of accepting invitations for days when he knew he would already have left, and not bothering to inform his hosts. Sometimes he invited others to dine, who only learned that he had gone away when they arrived.

14
The Mecca Gate at Jedda from the inside

In his earlier days at Jedda his European wife, the auburn-haired Dora, would come out to stay for a time, and, less often, he would return to their flat in London, in an old-fashioned block in Drayton Gardens, a home in sharp contrast to his large, rambling Turco-Indian house in Jedda, called Bait Baghdadi. He favoured simple local dishes, eating unambiguously, and his clothes were usually shabby. Sometimes he would emerge to join a team of British and Indians in Jedda playing cricket against sailors from a visiting battleship. Then, it used to be seen, he was a particularly aggressive wicket-keeper, rather less so as batsman.

In mid-summer 1930, he flitted in his secretive way from Jedda to Mecca, on becoming a Muslim. His conversion hardly astonished those who knew him best. It fitted with his characteristic of wanting to be different from his fellows, and surprising them. Ibn Saud later said, without naming him, though clearly referring to Philby, 'We cannot understand any man changing the religion into which he is born, even though we believe Islam is the best religion.' While not raising an objection, the King was unenthusiastic about his conversion.

When he returned from Mecca he presented to a friend in Jedda a long valedictory poem he had been preparing while waiting to go, dating it the 26 August, 1930. His manuscript writing showed the peculiarity of an increasingly wide left-hand margin until, by the bottom of the page, it was very wide indeed.

15
Philby's house in the Jarwal Quarter of Mecca

While in Jedda he kept two Arabian baboons, called by him Daphne and Stephen, of whom he was fond, taking them fruit at the end of every meal. When he went to Mecca they and their offspring seemed to miss him, and behaving rather badly were peppered with a pea-shooter by a guest left in his house. The baboons went berserk, wrecked Philby's study and, led by Stephen, held all at bay. A call was put through to Philby in Mecca, who advised asking the Russian doctor in Jedda to inject bananas with a sleeping draught, and on no account shooting Stephen. All refused the bananas except the youngest, on whom they had no effect, and the whole family broke away to take up a defensive position on the town wall for the night, whence it returned in calmer mood about the time of the dawn prayers.

With the help of the Dutch Minister the baboons were transported to the Zoo in Amsterdam; and when visited there by Philby several years later still remembered him, so he said.

His business enterprises, one was the agency for Ford Motor cars, were in time mostly sold out by him, though he took the opportunity of assisting an American oil company seeking a concession and outmanoeuvred the contending British company, which in any case was only offering very modest financial terms for what turned out to be a vast field.

Ibn Saud had put him on his payroll at something like fifty sovereigns a month, but Philby always maintained that he had refused to draw any of it. Apart from tiffs with the King, he was devoted to his good cause and country. Barren as most of the land was, it held him in spell, so long as it was unknown. Even in Jedda he would show sometimes a surprising attentiveness and willingness in guiding European visitors through its intricate bazaars, loaded up with exotic merchandise intended for or sold by pilgrims from Asia and Africa. He seemed happy then, but later was less so, spending more time in Riyadh or Mecca.

He took an Arab wife and had two boys by her rather late in life, having had affairs with other Arab girls earlier.

Once he tried, most unsuccessfully, standing for the British Parliament.

When the 1939 war began he was in England and found difficulty in obtaining a passage to Arabia. Already such matters were under Government control. It was then that Philby made an extraordinary proposition to Dr. Weizmann, the Zionist leader. Given £20,000,000 with which to compensate displaced Arabs, Ibn Saud could be persuaded to agree to Zionist plans for establishing Israel in Palestine. Weizmann

16
Philby with Ibn Saud in Amîr Saud's tent in 1933

was delighted. For such an objective it would be easy to raise the sum. Philby obtained his passage and set off to put his plan to Ibn Saud, or so he wrote to Dr. Weizmann, though he knew better than to expect the King would ever agree. Possibly it was only his way of ensuring a passage to Arabia, and perhaps later to America. He certainly deluded Dr. Weizmann, who later frankly admitted it.

When Philby arrived to see Ibn Saud at this period, in the first winter of the war, he indulged himself in making a prophecy once more.

Ibn Saud had been in the desert and on his way back to his capital met Philby coming up from the coast, who told him of the plan to 'compensate' him. In whatever form it was put, Ibn Saud, gravely upset, told Philby never to mention it again to anybody

When a short time later Philby insisted upon leaving for America, where he said he was to give lectures, it was against the advice of both the King and Saud. He would almost certainly run into trouble if he did go away from them.

From his way out of the Arab area, in India, he was sent to England. He died in the Lebanon aged seventy-five in 1960, surviving by a few years his friend, and in some sort protector and patron, Ibn Saud.

Faraway Arabia was a refuge and provided a cause for him, but the imp within him was not to be gainsaid, even there.

17
Philby with his jeep during his last expedition into Central Arabia

Philby's last important journey in Arabia was made with three Belgian scholars from Louvain University; Professors G. and J. Ryckmans, whose subsequent book called *Expédition en Arabie Centrale*, was published under the name of the third Belgian, Professor Philippe Lippens, in Paris in 1956. The journey was in part across unknown territory with the aims of geographical discovery and the collection and recording of rock drawings and inscriptions; in an area that had once been inhabited by Sabaean, Minaean and Qatabanite peoples. Philby himself had collected inscriptions nearby in the past. The expedition set out with the full permission and protection of Ibn Saud and was able to copy and interpret twelve hundred inscriptions, later published by the Ryckmans, whose book was illustrated with coloured and black and white photographs and the whole admirably presented by the author and the firm of Adrien-Maisonneuve. Philby's own work is comparatively short, though it represents his serious and painstaking study of all that can be gathered from all the known sources on the Queen believed to have been loved by King Solomon.

Gerald de Gaury

1 *The Bible Record*

The earliest surviving account of the visit of the Queen of Sheba to King Solomon is the one familiar to Western readers from the Old Testament: the passage which occurs in I Kings 10:1-13. It is reproduced almost word for word in II Chronicles 9:1-12. The respective dates for these compilations are probably 535 and 332 B.C., though it is clear that the material used was drawn from much older texts, some perhaps contemporaneous with the events they describe during the reign of Solomon about four hundred years earlier than the writing of the First Book of Kings.

Detailed court and administrative records and chronicles were generally kept in the palaces of the Near and Middle East, as we know from archaeological evidence, and we have an example of one such record being consulted by King Ahasuerus, the Persian ruler who probably succeeded Darius I and who is better known to history as Xerxes I (485-465 B.C.), in the Book of Esther (6:1-2):

> On that night could not the king sleep; and he commanded to bring the book of records of the chronicles, and they were read before the king. And it was found written that Mordecai . . .

Archives like these are long since lost to history, with their nature and contents, but the books of Kings and Chronicles contain reference to the earlier records on which they drew for their material. The Old Testament account of the Queen of Sheba's visit to Solomon certainly bears the stamp of having been based on a formal, contemporary record of a memorable court occasion: the state visit by a neighbouring sovereign to the greatest king of the day. Its authenticity is given further support by the fact that it is set side by side with an account of Solomon's relations with another local ruler, King Hiram of Tyre (see

especially I Kings 9:11-28), who similarly cooperated in adding wordly riches to the proverbial wisdom of Solomon.

In the Kings and Chronicles records of the Queen of Sheba's visit there is no hint of sensationalism, nothing to provide a foundation or justification for the legends and fables which had come to be woven about her name by a millennium later (and that are the subject of the main body of this book). To give it a clear perspective at the outset, it is therefore necessary to set down the bible story as this was placed on record by the compilers of Jewish history:

1
The imprint of the Royal Seal of Darius

2
An inscription in Persian cuneiform script giving the titles of Xerxes King of Persia

Now when the queen of Sheba heard of the fame of Solomon *concerning the name of the Lord*, she came to (Jerusalem to) test him with hard questions. *She came to Jerusalem with* (having) a very great retinue, *with* (and) camels bearing spices, and very much gold and precious stones; *and* when she came to Solomon, she told all that was on her mind. And Solomon answered all her questions; there was nothing hidden from *the king* (Solomon) which he could not explain to her. And when the queen of Sheba had seen *all* the wisdom of Solomon, the house that he had built, the food of his table, and the seating of his officials, and the attendance of his servants, (and) their clothing, his cupbearers, and his burnt offerings which he offered at the house of the Lord, there was no more spirit in her.

And she said to the king, 'The report was true which I heard in my own land of your affairs, and of your wisdom, but I did not believe the reports until I came and my own eyes had seen it; and behold, *the* half (the greatness of your wisdom) was not told me; *your wisdom and prosperity* (you) surpass the report which I heard.

'Happy are your wives! Happy are these your servants, who continually stand before you and hear your wisdom! Blessed be the Lord your God, who has delighted in you and set you on *the* (his)

3
'The Queen of Sheba and Solomon' by Paolo Veronese

4
The Solomon panel from the Baptistry doors in Florence by Lorenzo Ghiberti

throne *of Israel*! (as king for the Lord your God!) Because *the Lord* (your God) loved Israel (and would establish them) for ever, he has made you king (over them), that you may execute justice and righteousness.' Then she gave the king a hundred and twenty talents of gold, a very great quantity of spices, precious stones; *never again came such an abundance* (there were no) spices (such) as *these* (those) which the queen of Sheba gave to King Solomon . . .

And King Solomon gave to the queen of Sheba all that she desired, whatever she asked besides what *was given her by the bounty of King Solomon* (she had brought to the king). So she turned and went back to her own land, with her servants.

Thus runs the simple story as related in the Old Testament in its two recensions. In the text as this is set out above, the Kings passage has been used as a basis, since it was the first to be written, but the variants are indicated thus: words or phrases not found in Chronicles have been given in italics, and words or phrases found only in Chronicles have been placed in brackets. The text used here is that of the Revised Standard Version. It will be obvious to every reader that the variations range between the minor and the insignificant. Even the gifts emanating from Solomon's bounty may indicate no more than a remission of gifts brought by the queen herself.

It is notable that while Hiram of Tyre is also often mentioned in these chapters, with or without his royal title, the name of the Queen of Sheba is never once given. Nor is there any suggestion of a specific location for the land of Sheba itself – 'my own land', as the queen remarked to Solomon. On the other hand, there are several references to the place or tribe of Sheba scattered throughout the Old Testament:

Genesis 10:7: The sons of Cush are listed as 'Seba and Havilah and Sabtah and Raamah and Sabteca; and the sons of Raamah; Sheba and Dedan'.

Psalms 72: 10 and 15: 'The kings of Sheba and Seba shall offer gifts . . . and to him [Solomon] shall be given the gold of Sheba.'

Isaiah 43: 3, 45:14: 'I have given Egypt as thy ransom, Ethiopia and Seba for thee [Jacob] . . . The labour of Egypt, and the merchandise of Ethiopia, and the Sabaean, men of stature, shall come unto thee, and they shall be thine.'

Isaiah 60:6: 'The multitude of camels shall cover thee, the dromedaries of Midian and Ephah [a son of Midian according to Genesis 25:4]; and they shall come from Sheba: they shall bring forth gold and frankincense.'

Jeremiah 6:20: 'To what purpose cometh there to me frankincense from Sheba, and the sweet cane from a far country? Your burnt offerings are not acceptable.'

Ezekiel 27:20ff.: Ezekiel's list of countries trading with Phoenicia contains: 'Dedan was thy trafficker in precious cloths for riding. Arabia, and the princes of Kedar, they were the merchants of thy hand: in lambs, and rams, and goats, in these were they thy merchants. The traffickers of Sheba and Raamah, they were thy traffickers: they traded for thy wares with chief of all the spices, and with all precious stones, and gold. Haran and Canneh and Eden, the traffickers of Sheba, Asshur and Chilmad, they were thy traffickers.'

Joel 3:8: '. . . and I will sell your sons and your daughters into the hand of the children of Judah, and they shall sell them to the men of Sheba, to a nation far off.'

It is obviously impossible to draw from any of these passages definite inferences to enable us to pinpoint the geographical location of Sheba in, say, Solomon's time. But, by the time the books of Chronicles and Kings were being written, there is evidence for the tribe of Sheba (translated into Sabâ in Arab legend) being well established in the southern part of the Arabian peninsula. They were already enjoying a dispensation which was to be legendary by early Islamic times,

5
The head of a man made around the first century B.C. and found in the cemetery at Timna', the ancient capital of Qatabân

and the sober facts of its history can now be traced in large measure from South Arabian inscriptions engraved on stone or bronze. Yet, even if the compilers of the Old Testament records were aware of Sheba or Sabâ as a prosperous kingdom of the south, it does not follow that their predecessors of the tenth and ninth centuries B.C. will have seen the nation of Sheba as existing in a southern context. The only clue we have is the presence of spice and frankincense in the catalogue of gifts, for these must both have been brought up from the south from the area of Qatabân and Hadramaut.

The connection of Sheba with the spice trade may have been no more than that the tribe were carriers, relaying northwards the merchandise entrusted to them by other tribes who brought it to their boundaries from further south. The mention of gold and silver must refer back to mining activities, almost certainly in the northern part of Arabia, or perhaps to imports from overseas. Intensive exploration in modern times has failed to turn up any substantial traces of earlier gold or silver mining further south than latitude 21°N, which lies far to the north of Sabâ's northern limits as these are known in history. By contrast, the whole area north of this latitude, and west of longitude 44°E as far as the Red Sea, is scattered with the remains of ancient mines which must have been worked out at the latest by 'Abbâsid times (A.D. 750–1100). The Saudi Arabian Mining Syndicate failed to find more than one mine worth serious exploitation. This solitary

6
A vessel containing a hoard of South Arabian coins and inscribed with the name 'Amyatha'

7
A Qatabanian votive sculpture of a ram made during the second or third centuries B.C.

specimen, called Mahd al-Dhahab ('the Cradle of Gold'), lay between Mecca and Medina, and eventually yielded net profits of some $20 million simply from working the half-million tons of tailings from which the earlier miners had failed to extract the precious metal with their relatively crude methods of smelting.

In the genealogies of the Book of Genesis, the coupling of the names of Sheba and Dedan as brothers, with two different pedigrees derived respectively from Cush (10:7) and Abraham (25:3), provides a further pointer to a northern provenance. There can be little doubt that Dedan is identifiable with the town of the same name Daidâ), which lies near al-'Ulâ on the Hijaz railway. The listing of the brothers' uncles, Seba and Havilah, suggests a similar inference. In the name of the nephew, however, the *S* becomes *Sh*. The Arabic forms of these names thus become Sabâ or Shabâ, and the Romans and Greeks retained the Arabic form in Saba, Sabaea and Sabaeus. On the other hand, the translators into English of the Old Testament kept to the Hebrew form, while the translators of the New Testament evaded the issue altogether by referring to Solomon's visitors as the Queen of the South (Matthew 12:42 and Luke 11:31). Josephus, the Jewish historian of the Roman period, also side-steps the issue by calling her 'queen of Egypt and Ethiopia', but seems in his account to be doing little more than paraphrasing the Kings and Chronicles traditions, adding nothing to the hard facts.

(There is one fascinating detail which might be noted here in parenthesis. In Genesis 25: 1-4, the descendants of Abraham and his wife Keturah are listed. Jokshar, the father of Sheba and Dedan, was one of her children, but another was Midian, whose five sons included Epher. Epher and his brothers were among the sons of the concubines to whom Abraham gave gifts (25:6), 'and while he was still living he sent them away from his son Isaac, eastward to the east country'. By a process of transliteration from the Hebrew ('Afr) into Arabic ('Afar), and thence into Greek (Op(h)r), we end with a vocalization of the second syllable which gives us a transformation of Epher into Ophir and the correct location for the gold mines of King Solomon.)

There are other geographical deductions that might be made from the biblical record, but it has to be said that none of them would be conclusive one way or the other in solving the problem of the whereabouts of the tribe or state of Sheba. On balance, the Old Testament evidence seems to favour a north Arabian setting down to the time of Solomon and beyond, until the tribe migrated southwards (probably as a result of Assyrian and Babylonian encroachments) at an unascertainable date. For the birth of the empire of Sabâ, evidence does exist

8
The northern end of the oasis at ancient Dedan

in the Sabaean inscriptions which date back to about 460 B.C., and of which many thousands are known to survive. The genealogical details which these and others give enable the details of the first Sabaean dynasty to be traced back to about 500 B.C., leaving a blank of only some three and a half centuries between then and the earlier time of Solomon. One of the surviving Sabaean inscriptions does in fact almost seem to span this gap, though it presents no more than a list of kings and hereditary ministers. At least, with its frequent recurrence of dynastic names, the list indicates the continuity of the ruling family of Sabâ over a long period; but it also shows that during this period all the rulers were men.

9
Tiglath-Pileser III in his chariot

Given the inconclusive nature of the biblical evidence, and the silence of history so far as the location of the tribe between the age of Solomon and the sixth century B.C. is concerned, we are left with nothing but secondary references to Sabâ in the literature of the countries which border on the Arabian peninsula. Here, again, the evidence is far from conclusive, though once more it would seem to favour a northern rather than a southern situation for Sabâ at this period. The first certain mention of the tribe in Assyrian records occurs in an inscription of the Assyrian emperor Tiglath-Pileser III (745–728 B.C.), two centuries after the death of Solomon. Here the emperor records not only an incursion into the territory of the Saba'aa (Sabâ), the Maas'aa (possibly Ma'âzâ) and the Tema'aa (Taimâ), but also the intriguing fact.that Zabibe, a queen of Mât-Aribi (the West-land, or land of the Arabs), paid him tribute, while another queen of the same territory, Shamsi, was subdued by military action.

10
A railway truck with passengers in the early days of the Hijaz railway

Since the second two tribes mentioned were almost certainly located in the north, Sabâ was doubtless in the same area. Taimâ was a stage on the incense route, which passed from thence through the territory of the Ma'âzâ tribe, still known by that name in the 1850s when Richard Burton was travelling in Arabia, though now more generally called the Banî 'Atîya. Perhaps the Assyrian and Babylonian monarchs were mainly interested in the area for the sake of protecting this important trade route against the depredations of the tribes. The tribes themselves would also have provided the camel caravans for this section, as, indeed, they continued to do until the building of the Hijaz railway and the introduction of motor traffic in our present century.

Over a hundred years before the reign of Tiglath-Pileser III, the emperor Shalmaneser II (858-824 B.C.) had occasion to deal with Yâkinu, a king of Mât-Tamtim (the Sea-land, or peninsula), who duly made submission and paid him tribute. Yâkinu's realm would seem to have comprised the hinterland of al-'Irâq, al-Kuwait and al-Ahsâ in northern Arabia. He and a dozen or so others of his dynasty may have been princes of Babylonian stock, ruling the desert in semi-independence, or they may have been a surviving remnant of the

11
A relief from the reign of Sargon II depicting a groom leading two richly caparisoned chariot-horses

12
Two soldiers from the army of Sennacherib

earlier Amorite invasions. His great-grandson, Marduk-apla-iddina II (Merodach-Baladan), was contemporary with Tiglath-Pileser III, and therefore with the two queens mentioned above. Both Merodach-Baladan and Queen Shamsi were still on their thrones during the reign of Sargon II (721-705 B.C.), the latter still on tribute-paying terms, while the former was not only again in conflict with his Assyrian suzerain, but actually succeeded in establishing himself as king of Babylon until about 708 B.C., when Sargon's forces compelled him to flee. In this connection, one of his inscriptions names the tribe of Tamudi (Thamûd) and mentions three other unidentifiable clans, 'distant Arab dwellers of the desert, who do not know governor or commissioner, and who had not brought their tribute to any king'.

These give no more than hints of tribal presences, and it is with another inscription of Sargon's time that the threshold of authentic Sabaean history seems to be reached with a mention of valuable gifts, including gold, silver and perfumes, received by him from an Arabian king named Iti'amara. And from the next reign, that of Sennacherib (705-681 B.C.), an inscription survives recording the sending of similar gifts with congratulations on various Assyrian conquests by another Sabaean king, Ka-ri-bi-ilu. Both these monarchs bore dynastic names, easily identifiable with the Yathi'-amar and Karib-il which occur often in Sabaean inscriptions.

It has usually been said that, in its early days, the Sabaean kingdom was ruled by *mukarribs*, princes who combined their roles of secular ruler with that of a high priest. As has been seen, the earliest likely date for the oldest Sabaean inscription as such is about 460 B.C., so fixing a date of about 500 B.C. for the names of the earliest recorded *mukarribs* and their fathers. Before this date there exists, from other

13
The Bellino Cylinder records the campaigns of Sennacherib against Merodach-Baladan and the Medes and concludes with a description of the building of the Palace at Nineveh

sources, a patchwork of the names of tribal rulers, with others missing because of damage to stone inscriptions. By utilizing informed guess-work, it may be possible to carry a knowledge of the Sabaean dynasty back to about 720 or 730 B.C., but even if this exercise is performed, there is still no means of knowing when, in the two-hundred-year period between the reign of Sennacherib and the first attested *mukar-rib*, the dynasty migrated southwards to establish the Sabâ empire of historical times.

14
An Assyrian helmet of the late eighth century B.C. made from iron and inlaid with bronze

As a matter of interest, the inscriptions of Sennacherib introduce us to no fewer than three more queens of the north, Yati'e, Telḫunu and Tabu'a. There is no mention of any queen in any of the South Arabian contexts, however, much less of the Queen of Sheba who visited Solomon. She will have belonged to a far earlier and long forgotten dispensation in which women undoubtedly played an important part in the affairs of the tribe. We have thus delved back as far as is ever likely to be possible in our search for the historical figure of the queen herself.

Yet the romantic story of her visit to Solomon caught, as it still catches, the imaginations of those who heard it, and it is only natural that the tale should have progressed to take on a life of its own, both in the records of the chroniclers and the story-telling traditions of the bazaars and trading routes of Arabia. It is also natural that various colourful and sometimes fantastic embellishments should have woven themselves intricately about the original narrative – an incident which may be taken as having been faithfully recorded from the court register consulted by the author or authors of the Book of Kings. To track down the origins of the variations current by the sixth century A.D., and to see what further truths may be embodied in the ancient legends, involves an absorbing quest for elusive material through a vast body of Jewish, Arabian and Ethiopian literature.

15
Assyrian soldiers from the reign of Ashurbanipal fighting North Arabian soldiers on camels

2 *The Qur'ânic Record*

In the pre-Islamic poetry of Arabia, there are only scattered references, all of doubtful date and authenticity, to the story of the Queen of Sheba's visit to Solomon. The first comprehensive version to appear in Arabic literature is that given in the Qur'ân itself, the holy book of Islam which was delivered piecemeal at various times to the Prophet Muhammad, and collected in a final, authoritative form during about the middle of the seventh century A.D. Thus some sixteen centuries elapsed between then and the event itself, and about twelve centuries had gone by since the Hebrew record in I Kings was first written down.

The adventurous progression of the story through the long interval must be left for later consideration. For the present, we are more immediately concerned with the legend's development during the early post-Islamic centuries. And, since the Qur'ân version is not only the earliest in time, but also the most authoritative from the religious viewpoint, being, for the Muslim, God's own word, it should be given in full to provide a basis for comparison with other versions. It must, however, also be emphasized that, while no statement in the Qur'ân is open to challenge or question on the part of the faithful, no statement from any other source necessarily commands an obligation of belief.

The passsages from the Qur'ân which have a direct bearing are to be found in two chapters: No. 27, *Sûrat al-Naml* ('The Ant'), and No. 34, *Sûrat Sabâ* ('Sheba'). The relevant part of the former runs as follows:

> The he [Solomon] reviewed the birds, and said: How is it that I see not the hoopoe? Is he among the absent? Verily I will punish him severely, or I will slay him, unless he comes to me with a clear excuse! In fact he was not far off, and said: I have seen something which thou hast never seen. I come to thee from Sabâ with true

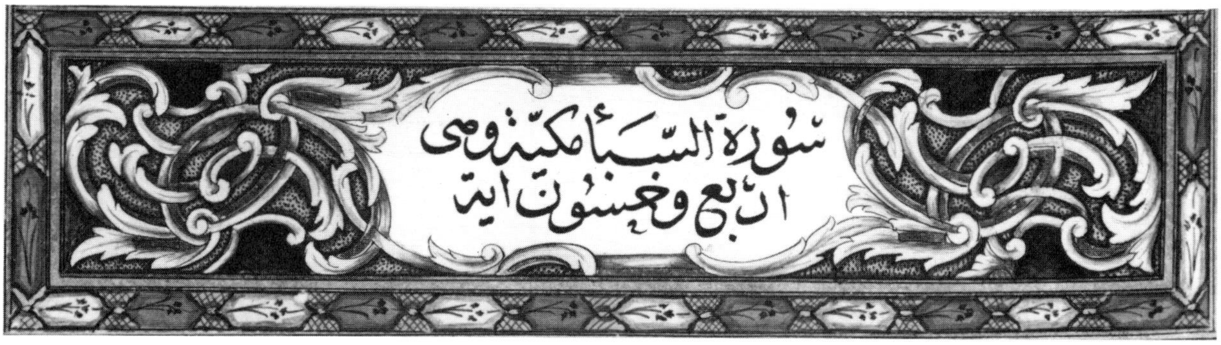

1
Two decorated chapter headings from the Qur'ân
a) No 27 The Ant
b) No 34 Sheba

information. Verily I found a woman reigning over them, to whom everything has been given; and she has a magnificent throne. I have found that she and her people worship the sun, to the exclusion of God: for the devil has taken charge of their affairs, and barred the way to their being rightly directed. And they do not prostrate themselves before God, who knows the secrets of heaven and earth, and knows that which ye hide and that which ye reveal. God! there is no god but He, Lord of the magnificent throne. He said: We shall see if thou has spoken sooth, or whether thou art of those who lie. Take thou this my letter, and drop it on them; then come back from them, and await their reply.

She said: O my people! here is a noble letter, which has been dropped on me: indeed it is from Solomon, and is as follows: In the name of God the merciful, very merciful! Be not rebellious towards me, but come to me submissively. She said: O my people! advise me how to decide. I did not wish to make any decision, except with you present. They replied: We have great strength and immense power; but it is for thee to decide. So consider what decision thou shalt make. She said: Verily, kings, when they enter a town, lay it waste, and humiliate the most noble of its citizens; yes, they act thus. So I will send him a present, and await the answer my messengers will bring back.

But, when he reached Solomon, he said: Did ye bring me riches, when that which God hath given unto me is better than that which he hath given you? No, keep your present for yourselves! Return to them; and we will come unto them with an army which they will not be able to resist; and we will expel them thence in disgrace and humiliation.

Then he said: O my people! which of you will bring me to her throne before they arrive to make submission? Said an 'Ifrit of the jinns: I will bring it unto thee before thou risest from thy place; I can do this with complete honesty. But one who had knowledge of the Scripture said: I will bring it unto thee in the twinkling of thine eye. So, when he saw it set by his side, he said: This is indeed by the grace of my Lord, to put me to the proof: whether I should give thanks or be ungrateful. For he who gives thanks does so for himself, while, as to the ungrateful, verily my Lord needs nought and is generous. He said: Disguise a throne for her, and we shall see if she is rightly directed, or one of those who have not been rightly taught.

So, when she arrived, she was asked: Is thy throne like this one? She replied: As if it were the same! and, if we had been endowed with knowledge before this, we should certainly have made submission! For she had been wont to worship idols to the exclusion of God, being of a nation of unbelievers.

She was invited to enter the courtyard; but when she saw it, she imagined that it was water, and exposed her legs. He said: It is but the glass paving of the courtyard. She exclaimed: O my Lord! verily have I wronged myself; and I make submission, with Solomon to the Lord of the worlds.

This, then, is the whole story of the queen's visit to Solomon as set forth in the Qur'ân, the only completely authoritative record of Arabia and the Islamic world. There is one immediately striking similarity between this and the Old Testament account in I Kings: neither mentions the name of the Queen of Sheba or gives any indication of the exact location of the country or people she reigned over. The Kings passage does seem to suggest a geographical context in its references to various products and the expressions 'my own land' or 'her own land'. But the Sabâ of the Qur'ân was evidently a people: 'I found a woman reigning over them.' (It should be said that, for the Arabs, Sabâ has in general always been a tribal rather than a geographical entity; and this impression is confirmed by the 'Sheba' chapter in the Qur'ân, which we will come to shortly.)

If, then, the queen's name and the location of her kingdom are left unspecified, the account in Kings is at least clear about the venue of her meeting with Solomon being Jerusalem; and there is nothing in

2
The Queen of Sheba exposes her legs to Solomon

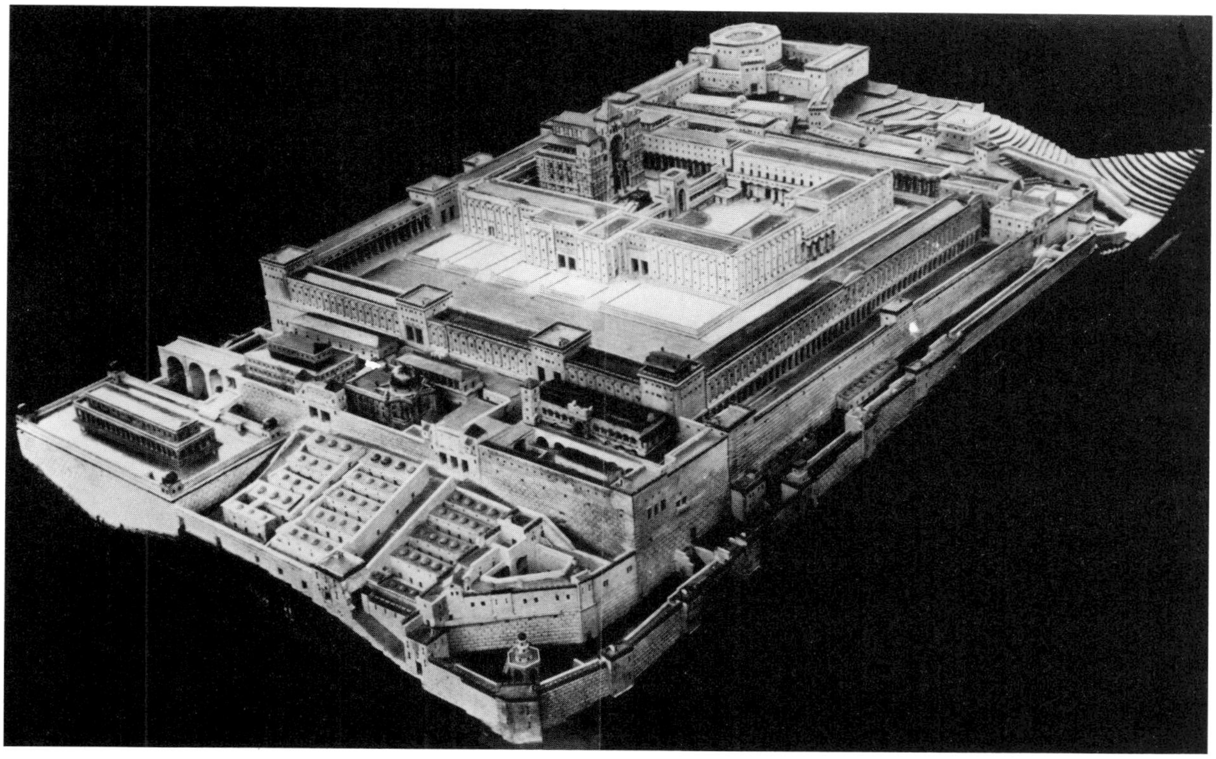

3
An attempt to reconstruct Solomon's Temple at Jerusalem

the Qur'ân record to suggest otherwise. The most obvious difference between the two would therefore seem to lie in the fact that the laconic court circular of the Old Testament contains no reference to the miraculous episodes of the hoopoe's explorations and the transportation of the Sheban throne from wherever the capital was to Solomon's court. Nor is there any reference in Kings to the glass paving of the courtyard, or to the lady's instinctive modest reaction on hearing of it and her consequent confusion. Kings also contains no mention of the queen's instantaneous conversion to the true religion, while the Qur'ân, naturally enough, avoids all reference to the Lord's special love of Israel. In the end, the most important difference between the two accounts seems to focus on the motive for the queen's visit: was it undertaken out of curiosity or out of fear? As the Qur'ân states it, the Queen of Sheba, for all her personal magnificance and state, was well aware of the superior might and grandeur of the greatest ruler of the age, known to command all natural and supernatural resources in the universe.

Equally, on the other hand, it is clear that Solomon was unaware of her existence until informed of it by a little bird; and had not apparently realized that the rich country from which, or through which, came the gold, silver and spices of Arabia, fell under the rule of a pagan woman. The shock of such knowledge, miraculously conveyed, was enough it itself to justify his issuing to her an ultimatum for both the furtherance of God's cause and the extension of Israel's empire over the rich lands beyond its frontiers. It is easy enough to believe that the queen would have been interested in riddles and 'hard

4

The Queen of Sheba comes to prove Solomon with hard questions

questions', which were at all times commonplaces in pagan Arabia; it is perhaps not so easy to credit the Kings suggestion that she was concerned to put Solomon's fabled wisdom to the proof. Yet it would be natural enough for a court scribe to have played down or ignored the king's summons, for the sake of representing the visit as a voluntary act of homage or courtesy.

On this question, the Qur'ân is decisive. The Arab queen, having seen that in this case discretion will be the better part of valour, visits Solomon of her own accord to answer his summons, and, being duly impressed, concludes that the God of Solomon is the God for her and her people, and hence makes formal submission. But we should also take note that, in neither of these two basic accounts, is there the slightest suggestion of impropriety between the two monarchs, much less of a marriage or of any subsequent consequences. So, it may be taken with Kings, that she 'turned and went back to her own land, with her servants'.

Again, however, we have to ask where did that land in fact lie? To help towards a solution, we may turn again to the Qur'ân, which, in the 'Sheba' chapter, tells us as much as is ever likely to be known about the Sheba of Solomon's time, which Matthew and Luke in the first century A.D. and the Arabs of the seventh century onwards naturally tended to equate with the kingdom of Sabâ and its capital Mârib in southern Arabia. How much support is there, therefore, for such an assumption in the most authoritative and earliest Arabic account. The relevant part of Chapter 34 reads as follows (verses 12–13):

Sabâ had for a sign in their dwelling-place two gardens, on the right and the left. Eat therefore of the provision of your Lord, and render thanks unto Him: a fine country and a gracious Lord! Yet they rebelled, and We sent upon them the flood of al-'Arim; and We transformed their two gardens into two plots full of bitter herbs and tamarisks, with a few jujube trees. Such was Our punishment of their infidelity! Do We punish other than the unfaithful?

Then We established between them and the towns which We have blessed separate towns, between which We provide facilities for travel. Travel then therein, by day or by night, in security! But they said: O our Lord, increase the length of our journeys between each and other. Thus did they do wrong unto themselves; and We made an example of them by scattering them altogether. Such then are signs unto those who have patience, and show gratitude! Verily Iblîs had spread heresies among them; and they followed him: all but a few believers, over whom he had no influence. But We were able to discriminate between those who believed in another world and those who were sceptical about it. The Lord is aware of every thing.

5
The Babylonian account of the Flood from the Epic of Gilgamesh

6
Noah's Ark as represented in an oriental manuscript

7
The southern sluice of the Mârib dam

The picture of the Sabaean homeland which emerges from this passage is clear: an Arabian desert oasis, with rich palm-groves, orchards and cornfields on each side of a wadi; and all this being overwhelmed by one of the disastrous floods such as have, at rare intervals, been recorded throughout Arabian history. Inevitably, calamities on this scale are linked in human reckoning with some offence by man against his Maker; and, in two cases, the view receives support from holy writ. In the first, the flood of Nûh (Noah) would seem to have wiped out the whole human race, except for a small band of the faithful left to repeople the earth; while the second, the flood of al-'Arim, evidently destroyed the premier tribe of Arabia and scattered its remnants through all parts of the peninsula. But there is nothing in the qur'ânic record of these disasters to help with pinpointing their location. Secular tradition places the flood of Noah in 'Irâq and the al-'Arim disaster at Mârib. The latter must obviously have occurred somewhere in Arabia, since Sabâ was certainly an Arabian tribe, but for stating where it could have lain no unequivocal evidence exists.

The arguments against Mârib as the scene of the second disaster would seem to be (a) that there is no mention of the destruction of a dam, or even of the existence of one, in the Qur'ân; and (b) that there is ample epigraphic evidence for the existence of Sabâ and the dam being in working order at Mârib from the fifth century B.C. to the sixth century A.D., when damage by flood or other cause was repaired

8
The northern sluice of the Mârib dam

by Abraha, the Abyssinian viceroy, in A.D. 542. This was many long years after the tribal distribution of the Arabs had taken shape. One tradition, as recorded by Ibn Kathîr (d. A.D. 1371) as well as by a number of the earlier historians, states that the Prophet once told an inquirer that Sabâ was the name of a man who had ten sons, six of whom (Madhhij, Kinda, al-Azd, al-'Ashariyîn, Anmâr and Himyar) settled in southern Arabia, while the other four (Lakhm, Judhâm, 'Âmila and Ghassân) established themselves in the north. It was a grouping that had long been in existence by the time of the sixth century A.D., though there is no evidence to suggest any date for the dispersion or its starting point, both associated in tradition with the flood of al-'Arim. If, as seems likely, the tribe of Sabâ was originally (and in Solomon's time) in northern Arabia, its southwards thrust could possibly have occurred some time between 650 and 500 B.C. Thereafter it was well established in the southern home with which Arab tradition has always linked it. Where al-'Arim actually was we must probably be resigned to never knowing.

Even so, there exists in the sober language of Kings and Chronicles as well as the Qur'ân the solid foundation on which the Arab and other historians have constructed, in successive stages, the fantastic legend of the Queen of Sheba's visit to King Solomon as it finally evolved. Some of the material which they used may well have originated in Jewish writings still available at Medina in the early days of Islam, such as, for instance, the *Targum Sheni* (*Book of Esther*), which was probably written in the sixth century A.D. And Jewish as much as Arab oral tradition, with adaptations by the professional story-tellers, must have contributed to the embroidery of the legend. All these points will need to be considered in the pages which follow. For the moment the immediate task remains to trace the stages of the story's creation through the work of Arab historiographers during the first five or six centuries of the Islamic era.

3 *The Early Historians of Arabia*

The romantic spirit of the pagan poetry of the Badawin tribes survived well into the Islamic era without discarding its oral dress. While the rocks and ruins of both southern and northern Arabia have preserved many thousands of inscriptions and graffiti in several scripts, eloquent of a literary tradition going back over many centuries, the central tract, which crosses the peninsula on a broad front of nearly three hundred miles between Medina and Najrân, is entirely devoid of such records, except for a few which may be attributed to southern or northern hands. The tribesman relied on the immemorial memory of himself and his ancestors, handed down from generation to generation with an inevitable accretion of embellishments.

The poems of the 'Ignorance' therefore largely survived in oral tradition, and only in 'Abbâsid times was the first real attempt made to collect them and preserve them in writing. Such literature as exists today was thus for the most part collected from the lips of men and recorded for posterity between A.D. 750 and 900 by a succession of scholars who were concerned to maintain the purity of a language which was already apotheosized in the Qur'ân. Given the nature of its origins, much of the matter relayed through the medium of human memory must always be treated with caution when it comes to considering it on a strictly factual basis. There are also grounds for suspecting that at least some enthusiasts who engaged in the task of collection and collation were at times tempted to pass off their own essays as the work of other more famous predecessors.

Be that as it may, the process of collating the remnants of the old poetry did not really begin until the mid eighth century. The task of collating the scattered utterances of the Prophet's inspiration into the form of an authoritative canon was, however, another matter altogether. In A.D. 633, the year after his death, the revolt of the false prophet, Musailima, resulted in his defeat at the battle of al-Jubaila in

1
A large block of sandstone covered with graffiti in the Najrân valley

2
An inscribed rock in the Himâ valley

3
Eroded rocks with inscriptions in Wâdî Halaqa

Wâdî Hanîfa, but at the cost to the Muslim cause of considerable losses from among the ranks of the Prophet's Companions, many of whom had been living repositories for his utterances. Abû Bakr and 'Umar ibn al-Khattâb realized that urgent action was essential if the words of divine wisdom were to be rescued from oblivion while men still lived who had heard them from the Prophet's own mouth. A considerable collection had been assembled by the time of 'Umar's death in A.D. 644, but another seven years were to go by before his successor, 'Uthmân, set up a commission under Zayd ibn Thâbit to establish the authorized version of the Qur'ân.

Next in importance to the Qur'ân itself come those sayings of the Prophet for which he did not claim divine inspiration. His surviving Companions and members of his family, to say nothing of innumerable others who had heard him talk and treasured his words, retailed his remarks to eager listeners. By the beginning of the eighth century, a vast mass of these *obiter dicta* was available, including, inevitably, the inventions or even deliberate forgeries of various interested parties. No fewer than 600,000 such alleged sayings were thought to be in circulation when al-Bukhârî (d. A.D. 870) and Muslim (d. A.D. 875) set themselves the formidable task of sifting the traditions and the authorities on which they were based so as to produce a corpus of the sayings which could be accepted as genuine, and hence an authoritative guide for the faithful over religious and social matters. The boiling down of the huge volume of reports to round about 7,000 well-authenticated sayings was a tribute to the devotion and meticulousness

4
The birthplace of the Prophet

5
The tombs of the Prophet's family

6
The Temple of Ilmuqah at Mârib, known popularly as the Temple of Bilqîs

of the two scholars. From the ninth century onwards, these two collections of the Prophet's sayings have been accepted in general throughout the Muslim world. Further collections of *obiter dicta* under specialized headings were subsequently attempted by others; but, by the end of the tenth century, the search for any lost residues of enlightenment ceased with the exhaustion of all available material. Since then, the works of Bukhârî and Muslim have held the field unchallenged.

So far as the subject of the present book is concerned, however, the important point to emerge is that, as in the Qur'ân, the collected sayings of the Prophet contain no mention of the name of Solomon's queenly visitor. Yet, well within the century which saw the birth of Islam, a name for this queen was almost certainly on the lips of the story-tellers, and the queen herself had become the heroine of a series of elaborate adventures, ancient and modern, including, of course, the Solomonic episode itself. And, it may be said, this name, Bilqîs, was no mere invention of bards, but an actual name, well attested to in the genealogies and histories of the Arabs, of a princess of the royal house of Sabâ who lived during the third century of the Christian era.

Since about the middle of the first Islamic century, Bilqîs has been inextricably associated with the Queen of Sheba who visited Solomon. When the name first appeared in the written records there is no means of knowing, for none of the earliest histories have survived the ravages of time. Apart from a few occurrences of the name in pre-

7
Statue inscribed Ma'dkarab found in the Temple of Ilmuqah and made in the style of the fifth century B.C.

Islamic poetry, it therefore has to be said that no evidence occurs for the existence of Bilqîs as a historical character, much less as a queen of Sheba, before the later ninth century A.D., when she is introduced to us by Ibn Wâdih al-Ya'qûbî (*fl. c.* A.D. 890) in a strictly fabulous context (see below, pages 67-8). Yet the legend of Bilqîs, as the heroine of the Solomon episode and other popular fables, must have been current in early Islamic times as a favourite item of the professional story-tellers' repertoires.

Not long after the publication of the authorized version of the Qurân, Mu'âwiya ibn Abû Sufyân conceived the idea of compiling a work on the general history of the Arabs. Apparently he engaged the services of a well-known *râwî* (story-teller) of the time, 'Abîd ibn Sharya al-Jurhumî, who had compiled a work entitled *A Book of the Kings and the History of the Ancients*. No copy of this has survived, though it must have been available to those who followed; and he is not infrequently cited by some later writers as their authority for the tales which they are passing on. It is virtually certain that the story of Bilqîs must have been included in this volume, and therefore a fair assumption that he should be credited as the first author to set down the tale in writing.

8
The Temple of Bar'ân at Mârib, popularly known as Bilqîs's Throne

The publication of the sayings of the Prophet was apparently discouraged until the reign of the Calif 'Umar ibn 'Abdul 'Azîz (A.D. 717-20), for fear that they might become confused with the Qur'ân itself. It must therefore have been at about this time that 'Urwa ibn al-Zubair ibn al-'Awwâm composed his biography of the Prophet, though he died in the year preceding the accession of 'Umar. Of this book's contents likewise nothing is known at first hand, though it must have represented an important contribution to the history of the time, the author's father being not only a prominent Companion of the Prophet but also his first (maternal) cousin, while his mother was a daughter of Abû Bakr and the sister of 'Â'îsha, the Prophet's wife. Such distinguished historians as Ibn Ishâq, al-Wâqidî and al-Tabarî are all known to have drawn extensively on this work, and he is also often cited as an authority. If he indeed touched on pre-Islamic history, as seems likely, he no doubt also relayed at least some episodes of the Bilqîs legend.

9
Two bronze plaques from the third century A.D. containing dedications to the moon god, Ilmuqah

To say that Bilqîs must have been mentioned by either of these two writers must, however, be admitted to be nothing but guesswork. Yet there are a number of specific mentions of the name in pre-Islamic poems, and these need to be considered, even though their authenticity has to be called into doubt. The following lines are attributed to Ab-karib As'ad, a Sabaean king whose reign covered the last quarter of the fourth and the first quarter of the fifth centuries of the Christian era:

Begotten was I by king of the kings,
  A crown'd head each of resplendent estate,
On women like Bilqîs and Shams; and springs
  The line of my forebears from Lamîs the great!
For ninety full years did Bilqîs hold sway
  Over her folk in all glory and might:
Her massive throne eighty cubits each way,
  With rubies and pearls and all jewels bedight! . . .

Another ode, attributed to the same monarch, does not mention Bilqîs by name, though the reference is clearly to her:

At Mârib my aunt did for me prepare
  A throne ancestral for kingdom rare.
There lived she years ninety, subduing the land
  From distant 'Irâq to the edge of the sand.
A thousand thousand her orders obey,
  Each ready to serve her by night and by day.

Both Nashwân (d. A.D. 1177) and Hamdânî (d. A.D. 945) quote a number of relevant couplets, attributed to another prince of Himyar in pre-Islamic times, 'Alqama ibn Dhû Jadan:

Where, oh where, are such remnants as these
  Of Mârib, the city of heavenly towers?
And Sirwâh too, and more mansions of ease:
  All built by Dhû Bata' for Bilqîs her bowers!

'Alqama has also been credited with the following:

10
'The Queen of Sheba' by
Edmund Dulac

Should'st thou ask of Silhîn and its days,
The days when 'twas Himyar that reign'd:
I would ask of Bilqîs, and her ways,
And her throne, red and gold intervein'd!

One further instance might be quoted, and this is attributed to Ahmad ibn 'Îsâ al-Ridâ'î al-Khaulânî, presumably a pre-Islamic poet, though little else is known of him:

The land where stand Ghumdân and al-Qalîs,
  Both built by that great chief of wide renown:
Yahdhibu Sharhun, and built too by Bilqîs;

The content and tone of these examples make it obvious that they were not the work of contemporaries of the persons or incidents they mention. At the same time, it is equally clear that if they were, as has been asserted, actually composed or even 'forged' by some other poet of the same period, they owe their inspiration to a legend of the Himyaritic age which was well established by early Islamic times. With the eighth century of the Christian era, however, we come to the threshold of what may fairly be called genuine historical research, inspired primarily by the natural wish to place on record all that could be garnered of the Prophet's life and work from sources then still available.

The first of the great Arab historians who lived and worked during this period was Ibn Ishâq, who was perhaps also the greatest in the long line of scholars who succeeded him. Once, when Ibn Ishâq visited the Calif, al-Mansûr, the latter's son, al-Mahdî, was present. The Calif, having introduced his son to the historian, then said, 'Now go and compile for him a book from God's creation of Adam to this day of thine!' So he went away and compiled just such a work; but, said al-Mansûr, 'You have made it too long, Ibn Ishâq. Now go and abridge it.' This he did, and the long book was consigned to the Treasury of the Prince of the Faithful.

All we have today of either the original or the abridged texts of Ibn Ishâq's history of the world is that which was collected and handed down in Ibn Hishâm's *Life of the Prophet.* There is, alas, no material relating to the Queen of Sheba's visit to Solomon, or to Bilqîs, among this. But, in the *Annals* of Tabarî (A.D. 838-923), an alternative version of the Solomon-Bilqîs story is put forward on the ultimate authority of Ibn Ishâq, from which it may be assumed that it was included in his history, from where it was extracted by Salamat, who passed it to Ibn Humaid, and from whose lips Tabarî had the tale. Assuming, then, that this story formed part of and was taken from Ibn Ishâq's history, it may reasonably be categorized as the oldest surviving version of the legend after that of the Qur'ân.

A stained glass roundel from the north aisle of Canterbury cathedral representing the arrival of the Queen of Sheba at Solomon's palace.

a

b

c

a Bilqîs, Queen of Sheba, with the hoopoe bird perched on the tree to her right carrying Solomon's letter in his beak.

b Solomon with his attendants, jinns, and the birds.

c Solomon's throne borne aloft by his jinns.

Bilqîs, seeing the fishes below the glass pavement, instinctively raises her skirts.

Overleaf Bilqîs and Solomon enthroned and surrounded by their attendants and the birds and animals.

a

b

c

d

Early Islamic maps of
a Arabia
b the World.

Sixteenth century Persian plans of Mecca showing
c the Haram and the position of the Ka'ba
d Mount Arafat surrounded by the pilgrims' tents.

An Ethiopian painting of the Queen of Sheba's arrival in Jerusalem and her subsequent entertainment by King Solomon.

Claude Lorraine's famous painting, 'The Embarkation of the Queen of Sheba', shows the Queen setting off to visit Solomon by sea instead of on the traditional camel.

4 *Enter Bilqîs*

According to Tabarî's version of the information supplied to him, Ibn Ishâq's account runs somewhat as follows. After the messengers have returned to her with Solomon's answer, Bilqîs informs her assembled ministers about how correct she has been in her intuition over Solomon and the absurdity of trying to oppose him by force. She has accordingly written to acquaint him with her intention of visiting him, in company with her vassal kings, so as to receive his commands and learn something of his religion. She then gives orders for her golden throne, decorated with rubies, emeralds and pearls, to be conveyed to a place of safe concealment in her palace – a place which is only approachable through seven gates, each beyond another and all of which are to be locked and bolted. Finally, she gives the viceroy who is to govern the realm while she is away the most strict instructions over the guarding of her throne against all intrusion and vulgar curiosity. Now she assembles her array for the expedition, under the command of 12,000 generals, each a king of the kings of Yaman and each having under his command several thousand troops.

Now, Solomon has dispatched several of the jinns in his service to bring him daily reports of her progress, and particularly to tell him what distance is being covered on each march by day or night. As soon as the Queen of Sheba's arrival is imminent, Solomon summons his human and superhuman advisers to make immediate arrangements for the magical transportation of Bilqîs's throne from her capital to his court.

With the entrance of the queen, the story in this particular version passes abruptly to the conversion of Bilqîs to Islam and her acceptance into the true faith. Then, towards the end of her state visit, Solomon approaches her on a somewhat delicate topic. 'Choose some man of your nation,' says he, 'and let me marry him to you!' She protests that it is, among her people, the women who do the marrying, and that she is above such things, being a queen with supreme authority over her subjects. Solomon counters with the argument that it is not so in Islam, and that it would be unseemly for her to ignore the ordinances of God. 'Well,' says she, in graceful submission to his authority, 'if it is absolutely necessary, I choose Dhû Bata', the king of Hamdân.' So Solomon joins her to the king in lawful wedlock, and sends the happy couple home once he has appointed Dhû Bata' to be his viceroy in Yaman.

Then Solomon summons Zauba'a, the ruler of the southern jinns, and commands him and his fellows to serve Dhû Bata' unreservedly in all that he may require in the line of palaces and other constructional work. So they labour unceasingly at his behest until the death of Solomon, the news of which is carried post-haste by a messenger of the jinns across the Tihâma to al-Jauf in Yaman. There the messenger proclaims in a loud voice, 'O ye folk of the jinns! Solomon is dead! Stop work!' So the devils down tools and betake themselves to two great rocks, on which they inscribe in Himyaritic characters the record of their labours up to the time of the first major industrial strike on record:

> In seven and seventy years we built Silhîn;
> Our sweated labour raised Bainûn, Sirwâh,
> And high Hunaida too, all in between,
> We fashioned with our hands, and eke Marâh.
> And seven-walled Qâ'a we made, and Raida's crown,
> The Talthûm fort. And, but for herald's voice
> From far Tihâma, had we left in Bawn
> The traces of our handiwork. Rejoice!

Thus the devils cease work and go home, while the joint reign of Dhû Bata' and Bilqîs comes to an end with the death of Solomon, the son of David.

But, besides Ibn Ishâq's version, there is an alternative narrative to which Tabarî apparently gives priority and preference. While this owes something to the Qur'ân, it was mostly drawn from a fellow-countryman of the historian, al-'Abbâs ibn Walîd, of Âmûl, in northern Persia, who received it at fourth hand from the Prophet's cousin, 'Abdullâh ibn 'Abbâs, a notable collector and purveyor of Arab legends. As might be expected, it is fuller and mildly more salacious than Ibn Ishâq's more matter-of-fact account.

1
Solomon commanding the jinns

Tabarî was born in A.D. 838, four years after the death of 'Abdul-Malik ibn Hishâm, whose historical work was little more than a commentary on the history of Ibn Ishâq, which he had the merit of preserving in large measure for posterity. Among other historians of importance in the same century, there was also Ibn Wâdih al-Ya'qûbî, whose history was completed in A.D. 832. Al-Ya'qûbî is remarkable for giving us a detailed if fantastic chronology for all the kings of Yaman from Sabâ himself, the founder of the dynasty. Calculating by averages for the reigns of these twenty-nine monarchs down to Dhû Nuwâs, the last of the line (d. *c.* A.D. 525), we have a dynasty that on its face value would have spanned some 3,400 years. Taking that with a due pinch of salt, the eleventh reign (a short one of only a single year) is of interest, since this was of al-Hadhâd ibn Shurahbîl, said to be the father of Bilqîs. His throne, however (and in what circumstances we are not told), was taken over by a usurper who reigned as tyrant for 400 years. But Bilqîs abided her time, eventually slew him and then reigned herself for 120 years up to the time of her affair with Solomon, who then himself took over the throne for 320 years. His son, Rehoboam, succeeded on his death for ten years, after which the line of the dynasty was restored to Bilqîs's first cousin once removed, Yasîr Yun'im, who was also her sister's husband and, incidentally, a well-attested historical king of Sabâ in the third century A.D.

The *Annals* of Tabarî stand as the fullest of the surviving accounts by the earlier Arab historians. Yet, though he opens his preferred account of the Bilqîs legend with a full pedigree, the name Hadhâd for her father is never considered. Some, he says, state that her real name was Yalqama, and he indicates an association with one of the more prominent kings of the Hamdânid era in recording opinions on who her father actually was. We can only draw from this an early warning of how intermingled recent history and ancient story had already become in the versions of the legend. But now Tabarî wastes no time into launching into the legend in his preferred version, which is clearly built closely about the Qur'ân account.

2
Solomon praying in the desert

As always, before he sets out on an expedition, Solomon mounts his throne and calls up his courtiers as well as the jinns and the devils, in that order of precedence, to take their places, each category behind the other, on chairs ranged on either side of his throne. He next summons the birds to shade the assembled company with their wings; and then whistles for the wind to transport them all forthwith to their destination (a matter of months away by camel back). The journey is performed in complete comfort and under ideal meteorological conditions – 'neither storm nor calm, but somewhere between the two'.

On such occasions, Solomon invariably selects one of the birds to be commander of his flying corps; and, whenever he needs information on any point, will turn to this officer to supply it. Landing somewhere in the wilderness, his first concern is for the party's water supply; and he makes inquiries as to the distance they are from the closest well. When, in turn, the men, jinns and devils confess to complete ignorance of the local geography, he loses his temper, declaring that he will not move from the spot until he knows how far it is to the nearest water. The devils, doubtless apprehensive of the torture of thirst, seek to appease their master, saying, 'Be not enangered, O apostle of God! If there is anything to know, then the hoopoe will surely know it.'

'Then send for the hoopoe,' says Solomon; and his rage knows no bounds when the bird cannot be found in his array. The punishment which awaits it will be dire. The other birds will peck off its feathers and leave it exposed to the sun so that it will never be able to fly again, but will remain permanently grounded like the creatures that walk on the earth. Or it will be offered the option of death, if that should be its preference.

Meanwhile the hoopoe is flying happily unawares above the palace gardens of Bilqîs, and being tempted by the rich verdure beneath, lands on the greensward, only to find another member of its own species.

'What art thou doing here?' asks Solomon's hoopoe of the hoopoe of Bilqîs, 'and why art thou so far from Solomon?'

'And who may Solomon be?' comes the pert reply.

'He is an apostle sent by God on a mission,' answers the visitor, 'and has divine authority to rule the wind, the jinns, the humans and the birds.'

'What art thou talking about?' says the mystified home bird.

'Thou has heard what I have said,' comes the reply.

'It is indeed a strange story,' the other rejoins, 'at which I am really astonished, for all these folk here are ruled by a woman, who has been

3
Two statues made from calcite portraying women with arms outstretched in attitudes of offering made in Sabâ during the second or first centuries B.C.

endowed with everything. You should see her throne: it is simply magnificent. And the people show their gratitude to God by worshipping the sun instead of Him.'

At this point Solomon's hoopoe remembers his master and flies off to rejoin him; only to be greeted on arrival at camp by all the birds with gleeful news of the punishment which he has in store. They repeat every gruesome detail, adding that the alternative of death is meant to ensure that the wretched creature should leave no posterity.

'But,' asks the knowing bird, 'did he not mention conditions?'

'O yes,' they reply. 'He did say unless thou hast a valid excuse.'

The qur'ânic phrases are now quoted as the bird's answer to Solomon's challenge: 'I have learned something which nobody knows. I have come from Sabâ with sure intelligence!'

And, once the bird has imparted the information which it has gathered from the hoopoe of Bilqîs, Solomon, as stated in the Qur'ân, says, 'Thou hast made thy excuse; we shall see if thou hast told the truth, or art merely a liar. Take this letter and drop it on them.'

The queen is in her chamber when the note floats down. Greatly moved by its contents, she places it in her bosom and sends for her throne and her lords. Again, as in the Qur'ân, she tells them that she has decided to send to Solomon a gift: 'If he accepts it, well, he is just a king like others in the world, and I am greater than he, and more powerful. But if he rejects it, then that will surely be something from God.'

Solomon's reaction to the gift is to issue his ultimatum that he will invade Sabâ. But the narrator also adds the picturesque detail of an unpierced pearl, which the queen has sent with a challenge for him to pierce it if he can. There was doubtless a *double entendre* intended here,

4
An alabaster male head from Sabâ, probably from the second or first centuries B.C.

but the narrator leaves it to be understood while emphasizing simply Solomon's perplexity. The courtiers whose advice he asks cannot help him, and he turns to the jinns, who do no better. But the devils are more cunning. 'Send for a worm!' they advise. And the worm, having been brought into the presence, takes a hair in its mouth and succeeds after a while in perforating the pearl.

When the passengers return to Bilqîs, she immediately assembles her array for a state visit to Solomon, who has proved by his rejection of the gifts that he is no common or garden king. In this she is accompanied by 1,000 chiefs, each of whom has an army of 10,000 men: an array of 10 million soldiers, going, not to fight, but to make an act of submission!

5
A selection of Sabaean coins
a) silver coins from the third to second centuries B.C.
b) gold and silver coins imitating new style Athenian prototypes from the second to first centuries B.C.
c) silver coins from the first century A.D.

Thus Tabarî brings us to the day when, having taken his seat on his throne on the occasion of some excursion, Solomon observes a cloud of dust in the near distance.

'What is that?' he asks.

And they answer, 'That is Bilqîs, O apostle of God!'

What a place for us to receive her in,' he exclaims.

There follows the qur'ânic story of the miraculous transportation of the throne of Bilqîs to the place of the queen's imminent reception, the man 'with knowledge of the scripture' having scarcely finished uttering his astonishing boast before Solomon sees the distant throne rising out of the ground at his side. His pious reaction to the miracle here carries a suggestion that he may have felt annoyed at witnessing this demonstration of miraculous power by someone other than himself.

Without further ceremony, Bilqîs is introduced and confronted with her own throne. When she realizes it is indeed the one from her palace she exclaims, 'But I left it in my castle, guarded by my troops all about! How has it come here? Now, O Solomon, I would put a question to thee, that thou mayest answer it.'

'Ask on!' he replies.

And she says, 'Tell me what is the water that comes neither from the earth nor the sky.'

Now, whenever Solomon is nonplussed his custom remains to inquire of his courtiers first, then of the jinns, and lastly of the devils. And, again, it is the devils who have the answer pat. 'Nothing could be easier, O apostle of God!' they say. 'It is the sweat of horses, set in motion by the action of their bile.'

So Solomon answers her, 'The sweat of horses.'

'You are quite right,' she replies, 'but now tell me what is the colour of the Lord.'

At this there is a great to-do, concerning which various accounts are reported by various authorities. One has it that Solomon is so shocked at the blasphemous nature of the question that he descends from his throne to prostrate himself in prayer; another that he merely faints and falls from his seat. Bilqîs, at all events, hastily retires, and the court guards discreetly withdraw. Then an angel appears before the king, saying, 'O Solomon, thy Lord would know what is the matter with thee.'

'She asked me a question,' says he, 'which it would put me to pain and grief to repeat.'

'God commandeth thee to return to thy seat,' the angel replies, 'and to summon to thy presence all who witnessed the incident, and to inquire of them regarding the question she put to thee.'

Solomon does as the angel commands, and when the whole company is present once again he askes the queen what it was that she said to him.

'Why,' she replies, 'I asked thee about the water flowing from neither earth nor sky.'

'Yes,' he says, 'and I answered the sweat of horses.'

She agrees that this was so.

'And what else didst thou ask me?' he pursues.

Promptly she replies that she has put no other question to him but that.

'Then,' he says, 'how was it that I fell from my throne?'

'That,' she says, 'is something perchance of which I know nothing.' (Or, alternatively, 'I have forgotten that.')

So he inquires of the guards, who corroborate her statement; and he turns to the courtiers, the jinns and the birds (though evidently not the devils, who might have been less tactful), and all aver that the single question she put to him was the one concerning water. At this point the angel repeats, 'So God commandeth thee to resume thy place, for God hath avenged you.'

Thereupon Solomon summons the devils to build him a palace, in which Bilqîs may visit him, and the devils take counsel among themselves, saying, 'Now Solomon is certainly an apostle of God; and it is true that God has subjected to him all His subjects. And Bilqîs is the queen of Sabâ. So he will marry her, and she will bear him a son. And we shall never be quit of this servitude.' Now they know that Bilqîs is a woman with hairy legs, and so the devils say to one another, 'Let us construct for him a structure that will enable him to see this defect in her, and put him off the idea of marrying!' So they build a palace of green glassware, with a courtyard paved with glass, fashioned to look like water; and under the glass they insert the creatures of the sea, fishes and so forth. When it is all completed, they invite Solomon to enter the palace, having arranged a seat for him at the far end of the courtyard. And, having taken his seat, he commands that Bilqîs be brought in to him. So they say to her, 'Enter the palace!' And, as she reaches the entrance, she observes the likenesses of fishes and other aquatic creatures in the glass. But, thinking it is indeed water, she instinctively lifts her skirts to make the crossing, and so exposes her legs and the downy curls which adorn them. Modestly diverting his eyes from the unexpected spectacle, Solomon neatly covers her natural embarrassment by crying out, 'It is only a glass-paved court!'

Whereupon she drops the hem of her robe, exclaiming, 'O my

6
Solomon and Sheba enthroned, the hoopoe bird is on the left of Solomon

Lord, of a truth, I have behaved foolishly. And I submit myself, with Solomon, to God, the Lord of the universe.'

Now Solomon immediately summons his council to consider the matter, asking, 'What is this blemish in her, and how can it be removed?'

'The razor, O apostle of God,' reply the human members of the council.'

'But,' he retorts, 'razors may damage her skin.'

When the jinns are asked for their opinion, they reply that that sort of thing is not at all in their line. So the king turns to the devils, who support the human remedy of shaving, which Solomon reacts to as before. In the end the solution they arrive at is to comb back the hair on Bilqîs's legs and apply to it a preparation of lime. By all accounts, this has the desired effect, though we are told no more about it than that Solomon then married her.

To round the tale off, 'Abdullâh ibn 'Abbâs is finally cited as authority for the statement that this was the first example in human history of the use of depilatory ointments. And so Tabarî ends on a happy note the story related to him by his Persian compatriot, and his history turns to a consideration of other matters.

5 *The Successors of Tabarî*

The first half of the tenth century of the Christian era was a period of intense literary activity, especially among the Arab historians. Tabarî died in A.D. 922, at the age of eighty-four; so it is probable that much of his work was done during the preceding century, though he no doubt continued to gather material until the end of his life. His works will certainly have been available to his younger contemporaries, and among these priority must be accorded to the famous geographer, genealogist and historian, al-Hamdânî , who must have been about fifty at the time of Tabarî's death, and who himself died in prison, where he was incarcerated for alleged heresy, in A.D. 945. Of Hamdânid descent, he had lived all his life in the Yaman while making extensive travels in other parts of Arabia.

Unfortunately, al-Hamdânî did not deal in any particular detail with the Bilqîs legend, though he contributed some significant points. He mentions, for instance, the name and pedigree of 'the most distinguished of the Yaman chiefs who visited Solomon in the train of Bilqîs', and adds a pedigree for Bilqîs along much the same lines as those given by al-Ya'qûbî, though with some minor differences. The real name of Dhû Bata', he says, was Bar-îl, and then he tells the tale of the marriage of Dhû Bata' to Bilqîs by Solomon, and of the latter's instruction to Zauba'a regarding the palace required by them, and of the strike of the jinns on the death of Solomon, all more or less in the exact words of the tradition attributed to Ibn Ishâq. The one original contribution which al-Hamdânî makes is in providing a record of the fruit of the union; and genealogical information supplied by him does have a bearing on the chronology of the period in which Bilqîs (or a lady of the same name) actually lived, though the historical Bilqîs was never a queen like Solomon's visitor, much less his wife, nor his predecessor on the throne of Yaman, which neither in fact ever occupied.

Al-Hamdânî's contemporary, Abû l-Hasan 'Alî al-Mas'ûdî (d. A.D. 956), tells us, by contrast, how Bilqîs bint al-Hudhâd slew her predecessor, Tubba' the First, before ascending the throne and ruling for 120 years. Then, in three or four lines, he dismisses the Solomon affair, along with the story of the hoopoe, by referring his readers to the account in the Qur'ân and other versions: 'Then Solomon reigned over the Yaman for twenty-three years, after which the throne returned to the line of Himyar . . .'

He does, on the other hand, make up somewhat for his lack of interest by incidentally drawing a new element into the Bilqîs legend: a strange tale to which various picturesque details were to be added later. Here it is, in its essentials, as he mentions it:

> There is a curious account, related by the story-tellers, of the appearance before her father, in the course of a hunting expedition, of two snakes, one black and the other white, of which he ordered his people to kill the black one. Then they tell of his encounter with an old man and a young man of the jinns, and of the giving by the elder of his daughter to al-Hudhâd in marriage, subject to certain conditions. Then she gave birth to Bilqîs; but al-Hudhâd failed to observe the conditions imposed on him, and she left him. It is a strange tale to be found in the *Book of the History of the Tubba's*, and, though we relate these accounts as we have found them in the works of the historians, we do so subject to our respect for the sacred law. Our version therefore does not follow the accounts of the ancients who did not acknowledge that law; but we adopt the treatment of the subject by modern authors who do respect it, and who admit the existence of jinns and the activities of the devils, as prescribed in the holy book, sent down to the apostle-prophet: in accordance with the evident proofs of its truth, and in view of the inability of later writers to produce the like of the Qur'ân, in which there is nothing false, either before it or behind it.

The chaotic nature of Arab ideas about pre-Islamic history in the tenth century A.D. will by this time be readily appreciated by the reader. The Arabs were for long unable to give the world even an approximately convincing or coherent account of the history of their forefathers, and one of the main reasons for their failure lay in the obstinate insistence of their historians on the identification of the historical Bilqîs with the queen of Sheba who visited Solomon in the tenth century B.C. It made nonsense of much Arab history. Yet, for a thousand years or more, the historians possessed on their very doorstep all the information they needed to bring their genealogies to life again. The records of Sabâ, engraved on stone, have even in our own century far too often attracted more attention from outside Arabia than from its own historians. In this matter, the tradition of discounting the value of the literature of the 'Ignorance', or of the Christian centuries immediately preceding the birth of Islam, has been the enemy of objective research.

The next historian to attract our attention for purposes of the present survey is Hamza al-Isfahânî, and he at least took the trouble to link his texts chronologically with the better known history of Persia. Interestingly enough, he seems to locate the original Sabâ ibn Yashjub and his son, who succeeded him during the first half of the fifth century B.C., making them contemporaries of Artaxerxes I (469-425 B.C.). Then, he says, after Himyar fifteen generations passed away before the unification of the Yaman under a single monarch; which would bring us down to approximately the beginning of the Christian era. This brings him to the reign of Hadâd, the father of Bilqîs, by the same route that was followed by 'Abîd al-Sharya and al-Mas'ûdî; and, like the former, he makes Bilqîs her father's immediate successor.

Hamza, however, is disappointingly brief in his treatment of Bilqîs herself, to whom he allows twenty years on the throne, as against 'Abîd's seven years and al-Mas'ûdî's 120 years. And, most astonishingly from our viewpoint, he appears to accept without question the story of her marriage to Solomon. On the other hand, he does add an element of interest about Bilqîs and her connection with the dam of al-'Arim.

The tribal tradition of Himyar represented her as having built the dam and a palace for herself in the Yaman. This, however, was strongly contested by all other tribes, who held that it had fallen into disrepair during the course of time, and that it had been Bilqîs who, during her reign, had repaired the dam of al-'Arim so far as this was possible. Some said that the dam remained in use after Bilqîs, until it was finally destroyed by the famous flood of al-'Arim forty or so years before the imposition of Islamic sovereignty on the Yaman in about A.D. 630. This would give us a firm date for the flood of al-'Arim at about A.D. 230.

According to Sabaean inscriptions, the great dam at Mârib, with which Arab tradition has identified al-'Arim, was built in about the mid fourth century B.C. by two successive *mukarribs* of Sabâ. Mârib

1
One of the early inscriptions on the Mârib Dam

then continued for centuries in full vigour as the capital of the Sabaean realm, the dam of Mârib serving its purpose into the middle of the fifth century A.D., when, in two consecutive years, 449 and 450, it suffered serious damage, either from floods or seismic disturbance. It was repaired by the reigning monarch, Shurahbîl Ya'fur, who duly recorded the fact on a stone tablet by the dam.

Nearly a century later, in A.D. 542, during the Abyssinian occupation of the Yaman, the dam again suffered severe damage; and the repair work, instituted by Abraha, the Abyssinian viceroy or ruler, occupied a vast gang of Arab labour, recruited from among the neighbouring tribes, for a period of two years. This was less than thirty years before the birth of Muhammad, and precisely eighty years before the consummation of Islam.

Within ninety years of Abraha's work on the dam, the whole of the Yaman had fallen under the rule of the Muslim Arabs. Yet no clues whatsoever exist to indicate how it was that this famous structure came to be regarded in so short a space of time as an 'ancient monument' – indeed, as one of the wonders of the world. It was probably man, not nature, who was responsible for its ultimate destruction and abandonment. The warring Arab tribes passed over the land like swarms of locusts, leaving nothing but ruin in their wake. And that is how Mârib has ever since remained: a wretched little village, sprawling hopelessly amid the monuments of a glorious past while the floods pour down each year past the temple of Bilqîs into the desert sands.

So far as the present inquiry is concerned, it may safely be stated that no evidence at present exists to justify the legendary identification

The sandstone country of north western Arabia known as the Hisma.

The pre-Cambrian granite mountains of the Hijaz, often called the Arabian Shield.

The ancient mine known as the 'Cradle of Gold' was rediscovered and worked by the Saudi Arabian Mining Syndicate between 1931 and 1946.

A Sabaean funerary monument from the first century BC.

a

b

Two south Arabian incense altars made from alabaster;
b was once the property of Philby.

An Ethiopian traditional painting of the story of the Queen of Sheba's journey to Solomon.

A late second century Palmyran sculpture showing the Roman style jewellery fashionable at the time and the manner in which it was worn.

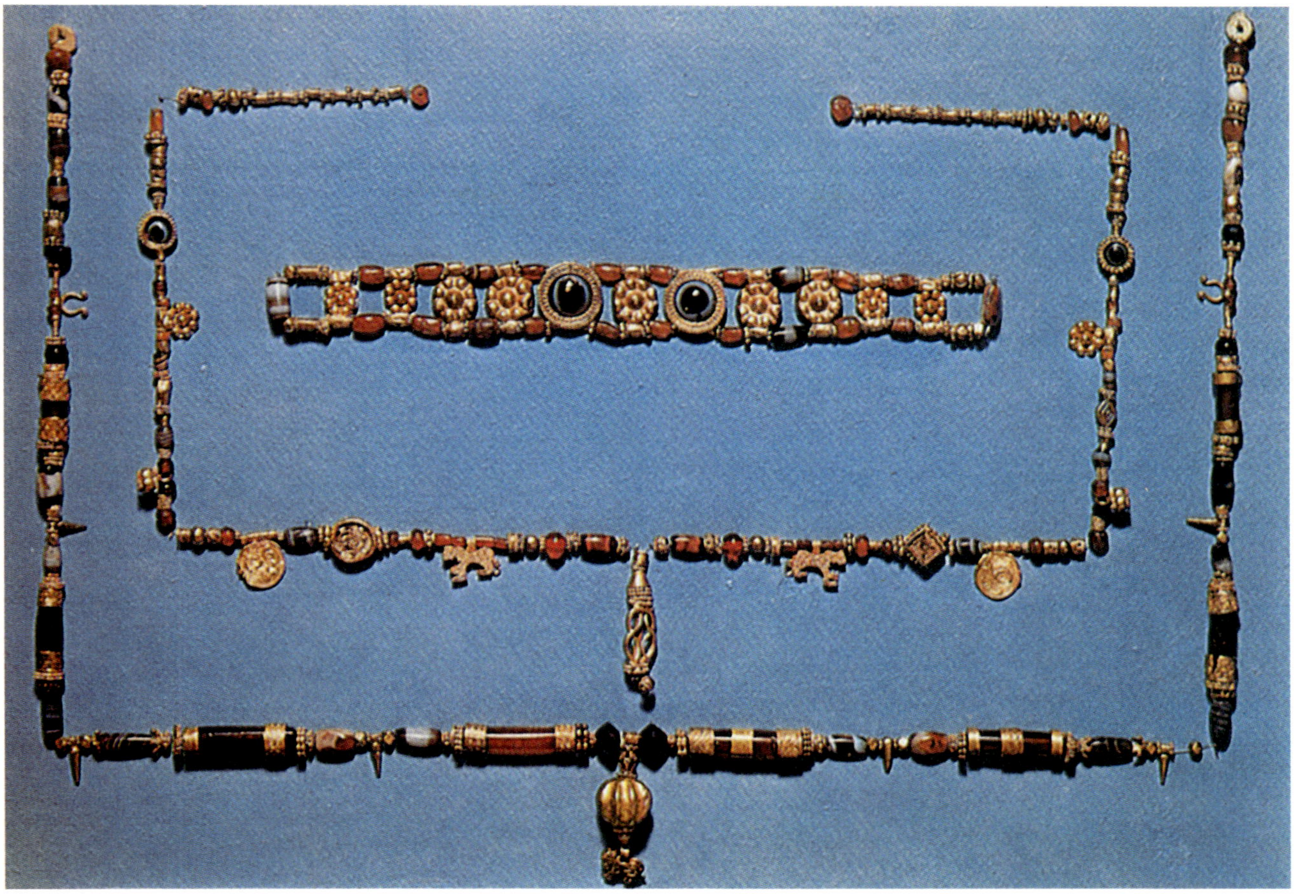

Two south Arabian necklaces and a bracelet made from gold, carnelian and onyx and designed to be worn together. Again the influence is Roman and the pieces were probably made between the first and third centuries AD.

A gold bracelet from the much earlier Achaemid dynasty. It is made from gold with griffins at each end and was once inlaid with precious stones.

A Sabaean votive sculpture of a bull caste in bronze using the lost wax process, again probably made between the first and third centuries AD.

A bronze incense burner with a figure of a mountain goat found in Mârib and probably from the third century BC.

of al-'Arim with the Mârib known to us from the records engraved on its ruined monuments.

The death of Hamza in A.D. 961 came three centuries after the disappearance of the last of those who held direct memories of events from the decade of the Prophet's mission – those who had been the eye and ear witnesses of Muhammad's public and private activities and of his 'table talk': the 'followers of the followers' of the generation privileged to see the birth and growth of a movement whose fundamental principles still, after fourteen centuries, powerfully influence the lives of some 400 million of the world's inhabitants. The century before the death of Hamza al-Isfahânî must have provided historians with plenty of time to ransack the oral and written records for all possible shreds of material which had a bearing on the romantic story of Bilqîs and Solomon. Before proceeding further in the exploration, however, it may well be useful to summarize those points on which the early historians are more or less unanimous:

First, Sheba is accepted without question as having been identical with the historical Sabâ of southern Arabia, having its capital at Mârib.

Secondly, al-'Arim is equally consistently identified with the famous Mârib dam, whose destruction by flood gave rise to the dispersion of the tribes of southern Arabia.

Thirdly, Bilqîs was the queen of Sheba who visited Solomon, and who married the Hamdân chief, Dhû Bata' Yanûf (or Barîl).

Fourthly, both Bilqîs and Dhû Bata' are firmly anchored, according to the actual Arab genealogies, in a group of historical personalities who can be assigned on the evidence of dated Sabaean inscriptions to the third and fourth centuries A.D.

Fifthly, Bilqîs is most traditionally regarded as having been the daughter of Hadhâd. (The name Hadhâd may even perhaps be associated with the legend of Solomon's hoopoe (*hudhud*) in Arab story.

The hiatuses in the time factor, to which the historians of early Islam were apparently so blind, seem crystal clear to us today. The Jews of Medina must have been familiar enough with the Solomon story, while the Arabs of the Yaman were equally aware of their genealogical records which the historians succeeded in carrying back into the distant past to forge links with the well-established history of their Jewish informants. Yet the popular fallacy that Solomon actually married the historical Bilqîs was never seriously questioned by the Arab historians.

2
Mârib today

The next authority on our list of witnesses in this *cause célèbre* was Nashwân ibn Sa'îd al-Himyarî, who claimed he was descended from the same ancestor as Bilqîs herself, and who was therefore familiar with the family history; and, since he died in 1177, two whole centuries separated his lifetime from that of Hamza al-Isfahânî. In speaking of his own relationship with his ancestor, he says without reservation that she was 'Bilqîs, queen of Sabâ, daughter of al-Hadhâd ibn Sharah ibn Dhû Sahar, who was mentioned by God, be he exalted, in the chapter of "The Ant" . . .' However, as we have seen, the name Bilqîs does not occur either in that chapter or in any other part of the Qur'ân. And, again, he tells us: 'When Bilqîs visited Solomon, he said to her that every Muslim woman should have a husband; and she replied that, if that was absolutely necessary, then [it should be] Dhû Bata' . . . and [it was he] who married her . . . Now it has been said that Solomon married her, but that is not confirmed.'

Here, then, we have a passage which seems to provide the most uncompromising disproof imaginable of the supposed contemporaneity of Bilqîs and Solomon, but Nashwân accepts without question the identification of Bilqîs with Solomon's royal visitor, though his claim of having qur'ânic authority to do so is scarcely justified. He also adds the detail of Mârib having been the queen's capital, and Mârib was, of course, the capital of Sabâ in historic times. There is therefore no obstacle to believing that the historical Bilqîs could have lived there. The name of the Mârib palace was Silhîn, famous in Arab story, the immense columns of which were more than twelve feet in circumference and still standing in Nashwân's time, though only to the height of a long spear protruding from the piled-up sand. And

3
Palmyra: the Main Square with the Great Colonnade and the Tetrapylon in the distance

Silhîn, we should remember, was according to popular lore one of the many palaces built for Bilqîs and her husband by the jinns under the orders of Solomon, though Nashwân does not include any mention of the incident.

He does, however, refer to the supernatural agency of the jinns in connection with the construction of a palace for Solomon at Tadmur (Palmyra), reputed to have been built of cyclopean masonry by Tadmur, the 'Amâlîq queen, daughter of Hassân ibn Udhaina. The springs and oasis of Palmyra must always have formed an attraction for the trans-desert caravans which plied between Babylonia and the Mediterranean; and, in 2 Chronicles 8:4, the actual foundation of a town on the site is erroneously credited to Solomon. The name Udhaina as recorded by Nashwân can only be the Odenathus of Roman history, who was made a Roman senator in A.D. 230. He was, in fact, the grandfather of the Odenathus who was made a consul by the Emperor Valerian in 258, and who was assassinated as the virtually independent monarch of the eastern marches in 167, together with his eldest son. The younger Odenathus, was, however, even more famous as the husband of Zenobia, who succeeded him to the throne as a consequence of the minority of their son, and who was destined to grace a Roman triumph in 272 after attempting an unsuccessful rebellion against the strength of imperial Rome.

4
A Palmyran lady of the late second century A.D.

5
The funeral bust of a Palmyran grandee

6
A Palmyran tomb carving showing a richly-dressed merchant surrounded by his family

7
A fourth century bronze statuette of a Sassanian king

On the face of it, the history of Tadmur and Zenobia would seem to hold out little promise of having anything much in common with the stories of Mârib and Bilqîs, but the Arab legends relating to these two queens do suggest some interesting points of resemblance and overlap, and may give certain clues to the complex intertwining of various strands which we will have to consider shortly. For one thing, Zenobia and the historical Bilqîs were virtually exact contemporaries in the middle of the third century A.D., and the Arab name for Zenobia was al-Zabbâ', meaning 'the hairy one', so providing an echo

8
A Sassanian glass bottle from the third to sixth centuries A.D. made using the Roman techniques of blowing and cutting

9
A Sassanian bronze helmet of the 'Spangelhelm' type

of the distress which Solomon felt on catching sight of his visitor's legs.

The fact that Nashwân's elaborate chronology places the reign of al-Zabbâ' in Palmyra some three centuries before the reign of Solomon may be noted simply as a point of academic interest. In life, Zenobia lived on comfortably into her old age as an honoured 'guest' of the Emperor Aurelian in a palace at Tivoli, the assassin of her husband Odenathus having been his nephew Maeonius. The contrast between the facts as these are known and the stories as they exist in Arab legend are clearly illustrated by the story of al-Zabbâ' and Jadhîmat al-Abrash, which falls historically within the last five years of the reign of Shâpûr I of the Sasanid dynasty (A.D. 267-72), corresponding precisely with the reign of Zenobia following the death of her husband.

According to unnamed sources drawn on by al-Ya'qûbî, the first of the southern Arabs to reach 'Irâq after the dispersion from Mârib was Mâlik ibn Fahm, who was not only welcomed by Ma'add and the other tribes already settled in the Jazîra district, but was invited to rule over them as one of the kings of the Persian sphere of influence. After twenty years, he was succeeded by Jadhîma al-Abrash, who lost little time in consolidating his influence in the area until he reached a district 'which was under the rule of a woman called al-Zabbâ' who . . . was extremely allergic to men'.

Addressing his officers on parade, Jadhîma announces his intention of offering marriage to al-Zabbâ', so as 'to add her kingdom to my own'.

10
A Sassanian silver boss with a lion's head in relief, possibly from a shield

'Obviously,' says his aide-de-camp, Qasîr, 'you would have the preference over all other suitors with her, if she were but of the marrying kind!'

So King Jadhîma writes to al-Zabbâ' to inform her of what he has in mind, and she replies, accepting his proposal. During the march to al-Zabbâ's kingdom, however, Qasîr makes a more determined attempt to dissuade his master from the enterprise he has embarked upon.

'Upon my word,' he says, 'but I have never before seen a bridegroom allowing himself to be conducted to his bride! Come, here is your mare, ready saddled. Mount her, and flee for your life!'

But the king rejects Qasîr's advice; and is in due course introduced to his bride. As she comes to meet him, she bares her leg in greeting.

'An ardent bride, you see!' she exclaims; and we are not told what it is that he sees.

But the king's answer comes pat: 'An ardent whore! A treacherous harlot!'

With that she kills him, and it is Qasîr who flees on the mare, back across the desert.

Following his escape, Qasîr goes to 'Amrû, Jadhîma's successor, and says to him, 'Do not cross me! I intend to slash my own nose and cut off my own ears. Allow me to have my way.'

And he carries out his act of self-mutilation before setting off again for al-Zabbâ's capital city. When he arrives there he seeks an audience with the queen.

'It was I!' he tells her, 'who counselled Jadhîma and his nephew 'Amrû to the point of making them kings, and you can see how I have been rewarded. Therefore I have come now to seek service with you; and, by God! perhaps we shall yet see 'Amrû slain by your hand!'

He continues to play on the queen's vanity until he gains her complete confidence; and she makes good use of him by placing him in command of her trading caravans. Voyage after voyage he brings back to her country quantities of the choicest merchandise, but the time comes when he visits 'Amrû again.

'This time,' he tells him, 'place armed men inside the cases on the camels' backs.'

And the caravan of 2,000 camels, each carrying two armed men in the boxes on its back, including 'Amrû himself, sets forth for al-Zabbâ''s capital. As usual, the caravan enters the city and the cases are unloaded before the houses of the various merchants charged to receive them, a number of cases being assigned to the palace itself. As soon as night has fallen, 'Amrû's warriors issue forth from their concealment and al-Zabbâ', together with a great multitude of her people, is slain.

So runs al-Ya'qûbî's somewhat laconic tale, which suggests no motive for al-Zabbâ''s hostile reception of Jadhîma in the first place, except for her dislike of the male sex, and which leaves unsatisfied the reader's curiosity as to what the doomed king saw when she uncovered her leg. Was it a drawn sword, or could it have been only hair?

6 *A Fabric of Fact and Fable*

While the Bilqîs legend had been developed by the Arab historians along its somewhat apocryphal lines, a more obviously fabulous element was, as we have seen, deliberately introduced into the story by Mas'ûdî on the authority of the 'story-tellers'. The tale was quite rightly ignored by his successors, with one exception, until the time of 'Izz-al-Dîn ibn al-Athîr (A.D. 1160–1234), a reputable historian who was to offer the world the first full account of the episode in writing. The single exception to the more general reticence, however, was Abû Mansûr al-Tha'labî of Mîshâpûr (A.D. 961–1038), most widely known as a literary critic of some distinction and described by Joseph Halévy as an author of 'educational romances' which were the 'forerunners of the secular tales of the *Arabian Nights*'. He was born in the year of Hamza al-Isfahânî's death and himself died long before the birth of Nashwân, so would seem to inhabit a historical vacuum, with no one to guide his studies and no rivals worth speaking of. His literary world was dominated by the formidable figure of the great innovative poet, al-Mutanabbiî, while the story-tellers presumably had the run of the baronial court of the Hamdânid, Saif al-Daula, at Aleppo, where he spent much of his time.

According to Halévy's redaction of the story which al-Tha'labî tells, Solomon, as the precursor of Islam, undertakes a pilgrimage to Mecca at the head of a mixed army, whose ranks include wild beasts. At Mecca he proclaims the coming mission of Muhammad as the greatest and last of the prophets who were foretold in the Book of Psalms. Then, wishing to see the Yaman, he one morning boards the wind with his followers, under the guidance of Canopus himself, and reaches San'â' at noon. The camp site being short of water, Solomon sends for the hoopoe to locate the subterranean water sources so that the devils can be set to work, drawing water for the party's ceremonial ablutions before the prescribed prayers. The hoopoe, however, is not

1
An inscription from the time of Anmar Yuha'min, son of Wahab' il Yahûz, King of Sabâ, of the Hamdânid dynasty 140 A.D.

to be found, and Solomon, in great anger, sends the sea-eagle to fetch him. Thus the story at this point falls into the traditional groove: the meeting of the two hoopoes in the garden of Bilqîs; Solomon's clemency towards the bird on its return; and his lending an ear to the news which it has brought him.

Particulars of the queen's life-story follow, on the alleged authority of one of the Companions, who claimed to have had them from the Prophet's mouth. Among her ancestors, we are given to understand, was one of the jinn community; and she attained to her throne by slaying her tyrannical predecessor, who had made a practice of dishonouring his subjects' women-folk. Her people once used to worship God, but it was she who had introduced them to the worship of the sun. She lived at Mârib, three days' march from San'â', and she sent gifts to Solomon to satisfy herself as to whether he was just a king or a prophet indeed. If the latter was true, she reasoned, he would reject the gifts, whereas a mere king would accept them. Among the presents of gold, precious stones and perfumes are a closed jewel-case, five hundred male slaves dressed as girls and five hundred female slaves dressed as young men. Solomon is required to determine the sex of the slaves without touching them, and to guess the contents of the jewel-case so that he might thread the unpierced pearl it contains.

The queen's messenger is received by Solomon with full ceremonial in the presence of a glittering gathering; and, inevitably, Solomon produces all the right answers to the riddles put forward. But he declines the gifts and asks the messenger to tell his mistress to come and see him, as a believing Muslim lady. Meanwhile her throne, though securely hidden in the farthest chamber of her palace, is miraculously transported by subterranean route to Solomon's palace by the archangel Michael. In this version of the story, when Solomon asks Bilqîs whether she has ever seen the throne before, he is moved

2
A pilgrim caravan near
Jedda on the road to Mecca

3
Mecca, showing the Haram

4
The old city of San'â'

by no more than the wish to test her intelligence, for the devils have been working hard to spread the rumour that she is stupid, that she has the feet of an ass and that her body is hairy. They have done this to discourage Solomon from contemplating marriage with her, for then he might pass on the secret of his domination of the underworld to any resulting children and heirs, and so perpetuate the devils' thralldom. In the event, her reply shows that she is in no way mentally disordered; and when she raises her skirts to cross the crystal floor, Solomon sees that she has legs of great beauty, with only a few hairs about her shanks, from which he modestly turns his gaze.

For Bilqîs there ensues conversion to the true faith and marriage to Solomon, followed by the subsequent building of three palaces by the jinns. But al-Tha'labî also takes notice of the alternative tradition, according to which Bilqîs married Dhû Bata' by command of Solomon, on whose demise the jinns ceased from performing work. And finally, and perhaps most importantly, he tells how, having lived seven years and seven months after these incidents, she dies and is buried in a secret grave at Tadmur. This could place the date of her death at about A.D. 430; and, he says, when her tomb was opened nearly three centuries later, her body was found to be in a perfect state of preservation. The calif of the day ordered a suitably grand mausoleum to be raised up over her remains.

5
A group of Parthian jewellery from the first century A.D.

While al-Tha'labî touches no more than most lightly on the fabulous origin of Bilqîs, and introduces a chronological element which fits the facts neither of Bilqîs nor of Solomon, he does raise an element of speculation with his mention of Tadmur in a context which might be expected to be more appropriate to Zenobia. In the meantime it is to the Bilqîs legend as presented to us by 'Izz al-Dîn ibn al-Athîr (A.D. 1160-1234) that we must turn next. And he introduces the circumstances of her actual birth with a prefatory warning that, while there is almost complete disagreement about the facts of her parentage, the story-tellers insist that her mother was a lady of the jinn community and her mother's father a king of the jinns. Her human father had married his jinn wife because he felt himself to be so incomparably superior to all other mortals that only a super-woman would be worthy of him. It has also been suggested, on the other hand, that his fondness for the chase might have led him into trouble with a herd of gazelles who happened to be a group of jinns in disguise. After he had considerately refrained from disturbing them at pasture, he was personally thanked and adopted as a friend by the king of the jinns, who also gave him his daughter to wife, against a dowry consisting of the south Arabian coast-land between Bîrain and Aden. But there is yet another story, which is evidently the one which Ibn al-Athîr considers to be the most authentic.

The father of Bilqîs, Il-Sharh, sallies forth one day for the chase, but has not gone far before he notices two large serpents engaged in mortal combat. One is white and the other black; and Il-Sharh, seeing that the black one is gaining on its adversary, orders his men to kill it, which they do. He then picks up the fainting white reptile and pours water on it until it recovers. After he has released it he returns home, and retires to rest alone in his private chamber.

Suddenly he sees at his side a charming young man, who makes haste to calm his alarm, saying, 'Fear not! I am the serpent you rescued this morning; and the black was a servant of ours, who went out of his mind, and slew some members of my family.'

The young man goes on to offer his rescuer the choice of wealth or a knowledge of medicine (perhaps meaning sorcery) as the reward for having saved his life.

'As for riches,' Il-Sharh replies, 'I have no need of them; and as for medicine, it is hardly a proper occupation for a king! But if you have a daughter, let me have her to wife.'

So the jinn marries him to his daughter, on condition that he shall in no way gainsay her, whatsoever she may do; and that, if ever he should do so, she will be free to leave at once.

6
The jinns

Il-Sharh is happy to accept the condition. In due time his wife conceives and gives birth to a son, whom she at once throws on to the fire. Horrified, the king nevertheless remembers the condition which was agreed and holds his tongue. When she conceives again, she gives birth to a daughter, whom she throws to a passing bitch which at once makes off with the tasty morsel. Still Il-Sharh remembers the condition to which he is subject, and again refrains from uttering any word of reproach or complaint.

Some while after these events, his wife goes with Il-Sharh and his army when he sets out on a punitive expedition against a rebellious vassal. Before long, they reach a vast, waterless desert tract, and push on across it once they have satisfied themselves that their water supply and provisions are sufficient. In the middle of the desert, however, Il-Sharh notices that all the waterskins are leaking badly and that the supplies of food have become contaminated with dust and dirt. Therefore the army find itself facing the prospect of certain death; and the rumour goes round that this is all the work of the jinns at the bidding of the woman.

Feeling himself unable to bear this final apparent outrage in silence, Il-Sharh seeks out his wife; and the pair of them sit down on the sand to talk.

'By the Earth!' he says to her. 'I bore with thee patiently when thou didst burn my son, and also when thou gavest my daughter to the bitch to eat. And now thou hast deprived us of our water and our provisions, and we are at the gates of death!'

'Hadst thou remained patient,' the woman replies, 'it had been best for thee. Let me inform thee that it is your enemy who hath suborned your chief minister, who hath poisoned the food and the water to destroy thee and thy followers. Come now, send for him, and let him eat and drink what remains of the water and food.'

So the minister is sent for, but refuses to touch the food or water; therefore Il-Sharh slays him where he stands.

The wife of Il-Sharh then guides the company to a place near by, where they find water and provisions in plenty. But no sooner has she led them to the place of safety than she takes Il-Sharh aside. 'As for your son,' she says, 'I sent him to a nurse, for her to bring him up; but unfortunately he died while with her. But as for your daughter, she is still alive!'

And, as she speaks the words, a little girl emerges out of the ground; and this is Bilqîs! But the mother departs for good, because of the broken condition, and pauses only to vanquish Il-Sharh's rebel vassal for him before proceeding to her homeland.

It is an absurd story, comments Ibn al-Athîr, of which there are many versions. But, as for the reign of Bilqîs in the Yaman, some say that she succeeded her father in accordance with his testament. Others aver, however, that he died without making any dispositions regarding the succession, and that the people appointed as king over them his brother's son, described as 'an abominable, wicked and dissolute man' with a penchant for deflowering the virgin daughters of kings and chiefs. When it comes to the turn of Bilqîs to fall his victim, he sends her his usual message and she gives him her own palace as a place of suggested rendezvous, while also arranging with two young men of her family to be in secret attendance. No sooner is the wicked king closeted with his intended prey, than the two young men rush in and slaughter him out of hand. Then Bilqîs sends for the king's principal ministers, to show them the tyrant's dead body.

'If there is any among you who respects the honour and pride of his race,' she says to them, 'see what I have done! Choose now some other man to be your king.'

'We will have none but thee!' they answer with one voice. And they make her queen over them.

In explanation of the visit of Bilqîs to Solomon and her subsequent conversion to Islam, Ibn al-Athîr relates the familiar hoopoe story, adding just one or two original touches. For example, when the story reaches the point where the hoopoe is found to be missing, someone suggests that he may perhaps have gone to see where the sun comes from, which happens to be beating down on Solomon's head, because it is the business of the birds to shade their monarch from the sun's rays. In this version, the episode of the glass-paved court is somewhat muddled, attributing to Solomon himself the idea of forcing her to expose her legs and show whether they are indeed hairy, in which case he intends not to marry her. The sequel presents no new feature; and we are told how Solomon makes the devils prepare the depilatory mixture, and how he does in fact marry her, and love her to distraction. In due course, he sends her back to her Yaman realm, where he visits her once every month for a sojourn of three days.

As he ends the Bilqîs story, Ibn al-Athîr makes a note of the alternative version, of the ending according to which Solomon, far from marrying her, suggests she should choose some man from among her own folk to be her husband: an idea which she initially rejects with disdain.

'But,' insists Solomon, 'that is the only way in Islam.'

So there follows the traditional account of the marriage to Dhû Bata', and of their return to the Yaman as king and consort. Silhîn and Sirwâh, Falyûn and Hunaida, are listed as being among the palaces which were built for them before the death of Solomon, after which they downed tools. So much for Ibn al-Athîr's version of the Bilqîs legend, from which he turns in due course to the story of Jadhîma; though this, as we have seen, also has some pertinence to our present study.

The classic account of the leper king, Jadhîma, is in fact that of Ibn al-Kalbî. He describes Jadhîma as the most distinguished and intelligent of all the Arab kings, the most valiant of them in battle and the first to weld the tribes of al-'Irâq into a unified realm. A chronology which runs true to form in its vagueness gives him a reign of 118 years, and this falls across the last half of the second and the first half of the third centuries A.D.

One fine day, Jadhîma sets forth, having decided on a raid against two tribes of Yamâma, only to have his advance guard wiped out by a rival monarch who has just conquered the same pair of tribes. Now Jadhîma takes with him wherever he travels a set of two idols, but after he has attacked the Ayâd encampment to console himself for his earlier defeat, a young Ayâdî, 'Adî ibn Nasr, steals the idols so that the Ayâd can hold them as hostages against further attack. Jadhîma promises that he will henceforth leave them in peace, and takes 'Adî into his service as his wine steward.

Now 'Adî is an intelligent and upstanding young man, and soon attracts the attention of Jadhîma's young sister, Raqqâsh, who promptly falls in love with him. One day she suggests that he should ask her brother for her hand in marriage.

'I dare not do such a thing,' he replies. 'I do not feel for you in this kind of way.'

Perhaps he is thinking of the wife he left behind in the Ayâd camp, but Raqqâsh is not be deflected from pursuing her suit.

'When he settles down to his next bout of drinking,' she eventually persuades him, 'pour out his wine neat, but let his companions have theirs diluted. Thus, when the wine has a hold over him, ask his permission to marry me. He won't refuse. His companions will then be witnesses.'

'Adî accordingly does as she instructs, and Jadhîma accords her to him in marriage. And he loses no time to repair to his bride to celebrate his nuptial night, from which he awakens feeling bright and well pleased. But his master, not feeling too good after the night before, asks gruffly after the cause of all this elation.

'The wedding of Raqqâsh,' replies 'Adî.

'So who gave her away?' asks Jadhîma.

'The king!' answers 'Adî.

'Adî takes advantage of Jadhîma's angry preoccupation to make himself scarce, returning to the Ayâd but dying shortly thereafter in a hunting accident. Yet Raqqâsh has conceived on her wedding night, and in due course gives birth to a son, whom she names 'Amrû. As soon as he has grown into a handsome youth, she dresses him in fine raiment and takes him to visit his uncle, Jadhîma, who takes the decision to have him brought up together with his own sons; and he has made for him a splendid robe of silver, with a ruff for his neck – the first such ornament to be recorded in history. But it is all too good to last. One day 'Amrû is spirited away by the jinns, and long, but in vain, Jadhîma seeks for him.

Many years afterwards, two men of the Qudâ'a tribe, Mâlik and 'Uqail, the sons of Fârij ibn Mâlik, are travelling from Syria to visit

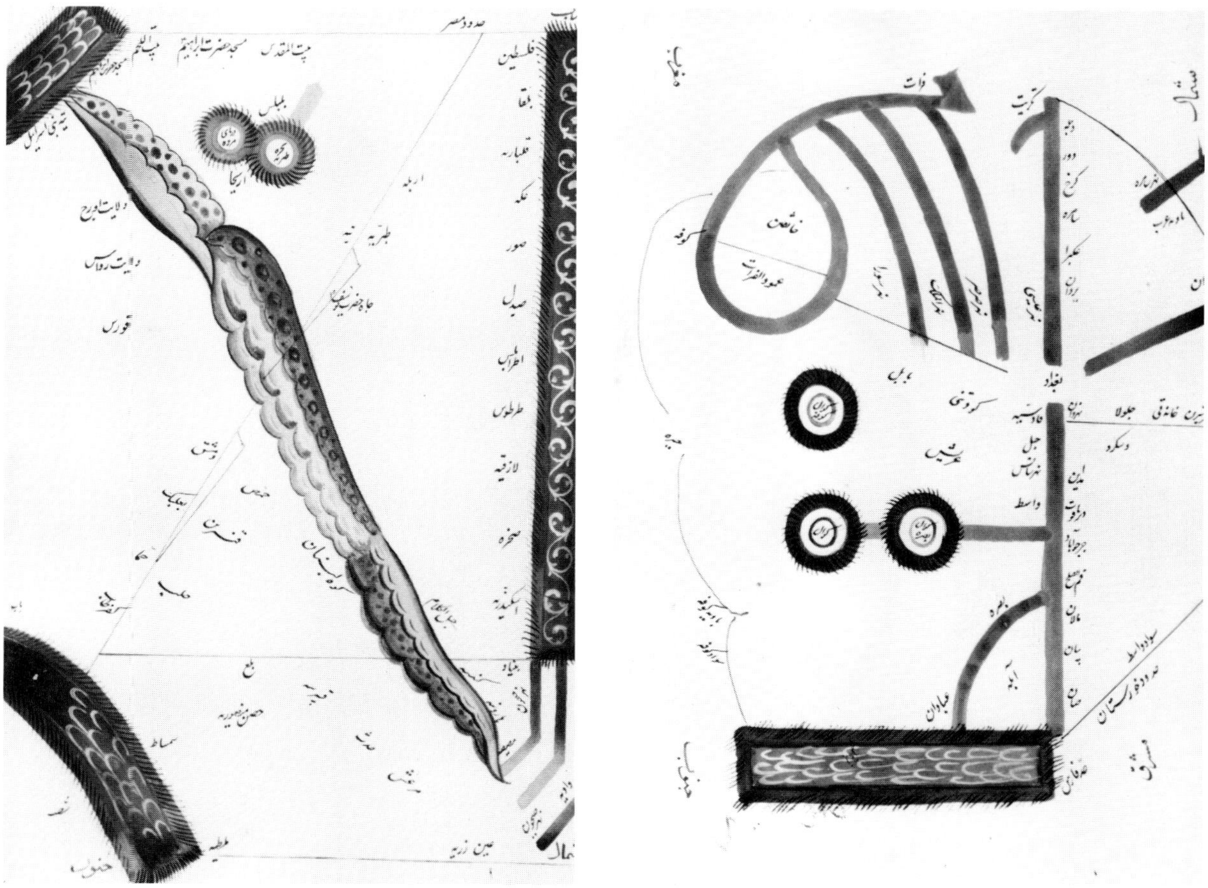

7
Early Islamic maps of
a) Syria and
b) Arab 'Irâq

Jadhîma with valuable gifts. They have with them a girl to cook and serve their meals, and one day, while they are eating, there comes into view a young man with matted hair and long nails who sits down on the ground a little way off, holding out his hands as if begging for something to eat. The girl hands him a sheep's knuckle, which he devours before holding out his hands for more.

'Give a beggar a knuckle, and he will ask for more,' she says; and it becomes a proverbial saying.

Then she pours out some wine for the other two, but ties up the mouth of the skin cruse; whereupon the visitor exclaims:

'O . . . does grudge me a glass?
For surely the wine to the right should pass.'

The two travellers, wondering at his ready wit, ask him who he is, and he replies:

'Ye despise me for sure: for my forebears ye sorrow!
Forsooth, I am 'Amrû, of 'Adî the son!
Of Tanûkh the Lakhmî my dam! and the morrow
Shall see me to war with Numâra be gone!

8
The Citadel at Aleppo has been fortified since the days of the Assyrians

At once the two travellers go forward to wash his head, minister to his wants and clothe him in new raiment.

'There can be nothing in the gifts we have brought for Jadhîma one half as precious as this, the very son of his sister!' they rejoice.

So they go with him to Jadhîma, who is overjoyed at the sight of his nephew come home.

'Forsooth,' says he, 'I saw him the day he left us, wearing his ruff; and since then he has never been out of my thoughts.'

But when they bring out the ruff to invest him, Jadhîma looks at his nephew and says, 'Why! 'Amrû has grown too big for his ruff' – another remark that became proverbial. And he turns to Mâlik and 'Uqail, saying, 'Name your reward.'

'That we be thy boon-companions for the rest of our lives and thine,' they reply.

Now, at that time the king of the Arabs of al-Jazîra (the middle Euphrates) and the Syrian marches is in a state of war with Jadhîma. Eventually, he is defeated and killed, and Jadhîma returns to his capital. But the defeated king is succeeded by his daughter, al-Zabbâ', whose realm extends from the Euphrates to Tadmur; and, as soon as she is firmly established on the throne, she decides to make war on Jadhîma to avenge her father's defeat and death. But her sister, Rabîba, who is a woman of intelligence and shrewdness, warns her against undertaking any such enterprise.

'If you attack Jadhîma,' she advises, 'he, too, may also in due course have his day. The course of war is full of uncertainties. Much better to use guile against the man!'

So al-Zabbâ' contents herself with writing a letter to Jadhîma, inviting him to visit her in her realm. She adds that she knows of no country in the world that has not declined in power and wealth when governed by a woman, and that she can think of no one in the world more worthy of her throne and her own person than King Jadhîma.

When he receives the queen's missive, Jadhîma does not attach much importance to it, but even so summons his counsellors. They, however, are almost unanimously in favour of accepting the invitation

9
The ruined gateway of the Nabataean city of Bostra in Syria

and annexing the queen's kingdom. The single dissenting voice is that of his principal aide-de-camp, Qasîr ibn Sa'd of the Lakhm lineage, the son of a slave-girl in Jadhîma's household, who urges him not to accept.

'No good my giving advice in the presence of the enemy,' says he, speaking another remark that has become proverbial. 'But write to her, inviting her to visit *you*. This she will do if her desire to make your acquaintance is genuine. Otherwise, take care not to place yourself in any way in her power. For, remember, you have wronged her by the act of killing her father.'

Jadhîma remains undisposed to listen to any advice of this nature.

'No!' he replies. 'Keep your opinion to yourself and do not publish it abroad' – yet another proverbial utterance.

Jadhîma does, however, feel it wise to sound out the opinion of his nephew, 'Amrû, who proves to be strongly in favour of the expedition, assuring Jadhîma that his own tribesfolk, who are subjects of al-Zabbâ', will most certainly rally to his side.

'They heed not the advice of Qasîr!' mutters the dejected aide-de-camp.

And the Arab bystanders retort, again coining a proverb, 'But the advice is on record.'

So Jadhîma proceeds to make all the necessary dispositions, naming 'Amrû to be his regent while he is away. The march begins, and when they have arrived at a spot called al-Fardha, Jadhîma takes Qasîr aside.

'What think you?' he asks.

And Qasîr replies, 'You left all thought behind at al-Baqqa!' – letting drop another proverb for posterity.

And when, in due course, the emissaries of al-Zabbâ' meet Jadhîma at the frontier with her greetings and gifts, he once again seeks counsel of Qasîr.

'Little danger but plenty of trouble,' answers Qasîr with another inevitable proverb. 'But,' he adds, 'when the cavalry escort arrives for you, watch carefully. If it draws up so as to lead the procession, then she means you no harm. But if it takes up positions on your flanks and rear, she will surely intend treachery. For this eventuality I will be riding al-'Asâ, a mare famous for her speed, all ready saddled and with all of your equipment.'

But when the escorting squadrons arrive, they draw up on either side of Jadhîma in such a way as to separate him from the famous mare, on which Qasîr is prancing about with a great show of style. As he watches him, Jadhîma is not lost for proverbial utterances.

'Alas for his poor mother,' he exclaims, 'yet what a man to bestride al-'Asâ.' And, he adds, 'He loses not the race who rides al-'Asâ.'

And even as he speaks, the spirited mare takes off across the desert with Qasîr on her back. They race ever westward, and she does not stop until she falls exhausted in the sand. But they have covered an immense distance, and Qasîr commemorates her last race by setting up over her grave a turret that is for ever afterwards known as the turret of al-'Asâ. And the Arabs have a proverb which says: 'Faster than the speed of al-'Asâr.'

In the meantime, Jadhîma has marched on, surrounded by the cavalry's 'guard of honour'. When he arrives in the presence of al-Zabbâ, she unveils to greet him, and, lo and behold! she is covered with hairs (*al-îsb* being the word used, and Ibn al-Athîr, our author, digresses briefly to explain that this word is particularly used of hair growing around the anus).

'Oh, Jadhîma,' exclaims the queen. 'A pretty woman, thy bride, is she not?'

This also becomes a proverb, and Jadhîma answers with another, 'It is the end. The earth is thirsty and the treason is clear.'

'By God!' she says, continuing in the proverbial vein, 'we are by no means lacking in consideration and good will, but it is honour that summons us to act. Hast thou heard that the blood of kings is avenged on a dog?'

The queen has the king seated on a leather mat, and calls for a golden bowl to be fetched, from which she gives him strong wine to drink until his head is swimming. Then she orders that his veins should be opened so that the blood will flow, but she is careful to push the golden bowl towards him. For, she has been told, should a single drop of his blood fall on to the common earth and not be caught in the bowl, she will be held guilty of his murder. As Jadhîma weakens with the loss of blood, however, his hand falls and several drops of blood are splattered across the floor.

'Let not a drop of the royal blood be lost,' she cries in alarm, too late.

And he retorts, 'No matter; the blood to him who has lost it!'

And that, too, becomes a proverb, and thus perishes Jadhîma.

'Amrû succeeds Jadhîma on the throne, after having to undertake a brief tussle for power, and once he is established, Qasîr comes to seek him out.

'Now make ready,' Qasîr says to the new king, 'and mobilize your army to avenge your uncle's treacherous death without delay.'

'And how, pray, am I ever to get at her,' asks 'Amrû, now in a position to make his own contribution to the proverbial sayings of

Arabia, 'so much higher as she is than the eagle in the sky?'

Now, after achieving Jadhîma's murder, al-Zabbâ' has taken counsel of a sorceress to seek insight into all her affairs, her future and her end. And, among other things, she has had her death at the hands of 'Amrû predicted, though her fate will depend on herself. For this reason she has become obsessed with a fear of 'Amrû, and has, as a precaution, had a secret underground passage built, leading from her boudoir to her castle. A further precaution she takes is to institute a search for a skilful artist, whom she dispatches in disguise to visit 'Amrû's court. The artist bears with him a secret commission to make portraits of the king, exactly as he appears in every conceivable setting, standing or seated, alone or in company, in armour or in disguise. The artist, having done his task well, then returns to al-Zabbâ' with his handiwork, and so she knows from the pictures precisely how 'Amrû looks without ever having set eyes on him in person. Thus she will be well equipped to recognize him on sight, and to take timely precautions against any mischief he may intend.

Meanwhile, back at the court of 'Amrû, Qasîr is urging his new king to undertake an act of mutilation on his body.

'Come, now,' he says, 'slash my nose and bastinado my back, and then leave me to deal with her.'

'I could not do such a thing,' the king replies.

'Spare me and it will be worse for you,' retorts Qasîr, delivering himself of yet another proverb.

'Well, maybe in this case you know best,' says 'Amrû.

And he proceeds to mutilate Qasîr's nose and to mark his back with signs of scourging. As soon as the deed is done, Qasîr departs hastily, as if he has entered into flight, proclaiming that this is the way in which 'Amrû has treated him, the former faithful servant of Jadhîma.

He comes to al-Zabbâ''s court and is admitted to her presence, but she, with her female intuition, suspects that there may be more to this than meets the eye.

'He has cut off his nose for some motive,' she tells herself, anticipating another proverb.

But she merely asks him how it has all come about.

''Amrû accused me of being responsible for the betrayal of his uncle by arranging his visit to you and encouraging you to turn against him. Therefore this is what he has done to me, as you can see, and so I have come to you, knowing that there cannot be one other on earth who will be more disagreeable to him as my protector.'

Apparently al-Zabbâ' then accepts Qasîr's story, and proceeds to welcome him with every sign of high appreciation. As she comes to know him better, she finds in him all that she most admires in men: courage and resourcefulness, much experience and a knowledge of the affairs of state. He meanwhile bides his time until he is satisfied that the pleasure she takes in his company is genuine and that he has her complete confidence.

'When I came away to you,' he tells her one day, 'I left all my possessions behind in 'Irâq, including stuffs of great value, perfumes and so on. Therefore permit me to go back now to recover them and bring them to you: articles of luxury, and materials, and merchandise of all kinds. My goods include things which you can sell for great profit and things which the kings of the earth would envy.'

On hearing this, al-Zabbâ' without hesitation provides him with money and arranges a caravan for him to lead; and with which in due course he arrives in 'Irâq. At the first opportunity he visits 'Amrû in secret, to tell him how things stand. He proposes that he should now equip him with a rich cargo of rare merchandise which he can take back to the queen, his enemy.

'Perhaps then,' he says, 'God will grant me domination of al-Zabbâ', and you will have the satisfaction of seeing your revenge fulfilled.'

Upon his return to al-Zabbâ', the queen is delighted with the results of his expedition, and after a while dispatches him yet again, this time with an even larger caravan train and even more ample funds. But on this occasion Qasîr fully intends to see his plan through to fruition.

'Collect together for me now the most trustworthy of your warriors,' he tells 'Amru. 'Arrange for large sacks to carry them in, so that each camel can carry two sacks. But take care that the mouths of the sacks are knotted on and can be undone from the inside. Once we are safely inside al-Zabbâ''s city,' continues Qasîr, 'I will post you at the entrance to her secret tunnel, which connects her private apartment with her castle. Then I will give the signal for the men to come out of their sacks, and they will call on the townsfolk to surrender, fighting only those who try to resist. And when al-Zabbâ' comes to the tunnel, you will be able to kill her there.'

In this way everything has been arranged by the time the caravan sets forth on its journey back to the city of al-Zabbâ'. And, as it comes near to its destination, Qasîr goes on ahead to bring the queen news of its imminent arrival with all manner of rich merchandise. Now it is the practice of Qasîr (and he, says Ibn al-Kalbî, was the first to adopt the tactic), to rest up by day and to march at night. Therefore he proposes to al-Zabbâ' that she should ride out with him to watch the camels coming in.

As the laden beasts advance towards them, the queen notices how deeply the camels' feet are sinking into the sandy ground. 'O Qasîr!' she exclaims:

'What ails the wretched beasts, they march so slow?
  Is't iron bars they carry, or great rocks?
Or solid lead, perchance, for all I know!
  Or men erect, or crouching in a box?'

When the caravan reaches the city centre, the camels are couched; and when Qasîr gives the signal, the warriors emerge from their sacks, shouting to the citizens and rushing into combat. Qasîr has meanwhile also conducted 'Amrû to the tunnel, where al-Zabbâ' soon appears, seeking her line of escape. But when she sees 'Amrû barring the way, she recognizes him instantly from his pictures and at once sucks a ring in which she carries a deadly poison.

'By my own hand, and not by the hand of 'Amrû,' she exclaims, leaving a final proverb that was current ever thereafter.

But 'Amrû draws his sword and slays her before the poison can take effect; and proceeds to lay claim to the city before returning to 'Irâq.

With the conclusion of their narratives, our historians pass on to accounts of the centuries which follow and which lead to the birth of Islam. And here we may leave them, Ibn al-Athîr and Ibn al-Kalbî, with a feeling of gratitude for the light they have shed, albeit without realizing it, on various aspects of these related legends which are engaging our attention. The very full accounts of the miraculous circumstances which attended the birth of Bilqîs and her pedigree on her father's side; the more or less orthodox treatment of the episode of her relationship with King Solomon; and the fine and vivid versions of the Zenobia/al-Zabbâ' story – all these are factors which contribute significantly to throwing light on the mystery of the two queens whose exploits in legend have thrilled audiences in Arab music-halls down the centuries to the present day.

7 *Later Contributors*

After Ibn al-Athîr, the task of refining the metal of history from the ore of legend becomes no easier for reasons which will already be more than familiar to the reader. As has been emphasized, the Arab scholars preferred, on the whole, to rely on their oral traditions when it came to marshalling fact and proof, especially for the genealogies, and they acted deliberately in ignoring the material that lay all about them in the form of ancient inscriptions surviving on rocks and ruins – these, of course, belonging to the pre-Islamic era of the 'Ignorance'. But, once again, at this point it has to be said that the many hundreds of names so recorded have never been found to include that of Bilqîs.

In the literature, however, we do not now have to look far before coming across a story that seems to have a recognizable ring to it. This is the account told by Ahmad al-Nuwairî (d. 1332) of Shamir Dhû l-Janâh, said to be a son of Ab-karib As'ad (*c*.370–410), a Sabaean king who had ambitions to rule the world. Among the expeditions he dispatched, it is said, was one to China, led by Shamir, which arrived in due course outside the walls of the city which we today know as Samarqand. Here Shamir lays seige to the town. But, meeting with no success in his probing attacks, he sallies forth from the camp to make a reconnaissance with his bodyguard. During the course of this patrol, he manages to capture one of the citizens of Samarqand, whom he is most careful to treat with courtesy and consideration. His tact pays off and he is able to garner much useful information. He learns that the local king is an ignorant reprobate, interested in nothing in life beyond wine, women and food. It is his daughter, unnamed, who in fact manages the affairs of state.

Once he has assured his prisoner of his good will, Shamir releases him and sends him back into the city with a suitable gift for the lady regent and a message to the effect that his visit to the country has been brought about only because of the reports which he has heard of her intelligence. He has therefore come to seek her hand in marriage, so that they may produce a son who is worthy to reign jointly over the Arabs and Persians. He has not come to seek any riches, he says; indeed, he has brought with him and actually has with him at that moment 4,000 boxes of gold and silver, and is even now on his way to the conquest of China. As he continues on his way, he will leave all these boxes of treasure in trust with her, only on condition that, if he find success in his conquest, she will become his wife; but that, if he perishes, the wealth will be hers.

She accepts his conditions at once, telling the messenger to press his master to send on the boxes without delay. And send them along Shamir does, but with two armed soldiers stowed away in each box. Now, Samarqand has four gates, and each gate has a guard of 4,000 men. Presumably, therefore, 1,000 boxes have to enter at each gate. Shamir has arranged with the boxes' occupants that the sound of a bell will signal the time for them to break out of their boxes and set to to overpower the guards and open the gates for the expectant army outside. And this is how he duly effects an entry into the city, slays its inhabitants and seizes all its treasures. What became of the lady and her dissolute father we are never told, but Shamir, it is said, then continued his onward march into China.

Al-Hamdânî, however, though he lacks the picturesque details, attributes the Samarqand incident to Shamir Yur'ish, an earlier monarch of about A.D. 300. According to this historian, once he has reached the province of al-Sughd (Sogdiana), Shamir finds himself face to face with the Persian army at Samarqand, takes the town by assault and razes it to the ground after having killed most of the population. Hence its name thereafter: Shamir-kanda, 'destroyed by Shamir', or Samarqand. The campaign is also mentioned in verse by Di'bil ibn 'Alî, one of the court poets to Harûn al-Rashîd (A.D. 786-809):

At Merv they inscribed their names on the walls;
  At Shûsh they wrote their deeds on the gate.
At Samarqand always the name recalls
  Of Shamir his balsams as they relate!

It is after this that Shamir then advances towards 'China', reducing the king of Sogdiana to despair until one of his ministers, more intelligent than the rest, thinks of a strategem. He slits his own nose and flees as if to the safety of Shamir's camp, some ten stages distant in the

1
An inscription from Mârib of the time of Ilsharah Yahdib and his brother, Ya'zil Bayyin, kings of Sabâ and Dhû Raydân, about 200 A.D.

tractless desert. There, complaining of the savage treatment he has received at the hands of his master, he offers to guide the invading force to its destination. As soon as his offer has been gladly accepted, he tells Shamir to lay in enough water for three full days' march, the distance of the nearest well that lies along their route. After they have travelled for the three days, the water supply is exhausted, but there is no well from which they could replenish it. The wily minister then confesses to the trick he has played to save his native land from an enemy, and the story leaves us to assume that he shares the fate of his victims, who are doomed to perish from thirst in the wilderness, as Shamir does himself.

Shortly thereafter, Shamir's son, Abû Mâlik, is preparing to avenge his father's death on the kings of China when his attention is diverted by the rumour of an emerald mine in the Sahara, in seeking which he meets his own end. And so it is to *his* son, known as Tubba' al-Aqran, that the task falls of avenging Shamir's death. He goes first to restore the great city of Samarqand which his grandfather once destroyed, before moving on to lay waste to the unnamed capital of the enemy, which he duly replaces with a new town to house the colony of Arabs which he leaves behind to garrison their newly won territory. Their descendants were still there in the middle of the eleventh century, according to al-Hamdânî, but the fact of the matter is that no independent or corroborating evidence exists whatsoever to vouch for the reality of any of these campaigns. Vivid and colourful as the events may sound, we cannot take them to be more than fictions of the romantic imagination.

The Sabaean kings probably never penetrated much further into the rival empires of Rome and Persia than the fringes of 'Irâq and Syria. Yet, in those marches, there lay ample material on which the propagandists of Arab virtue might work. The trick of the slashed nose and the 'Trojan horse' technique which was used to gain entry into Samarqand had already, as will be clear, offered a foundation for the Arabian version of the Zenobia legend.

There are, on the other hand, certain developments in the 'Irâq and adjacent areas which were attributed by Ibn Miskawaih to the reigns of Ab-karib As'ad and his sons, though it would seem, from internal evidence, that they should more convincingly be linked with the military activities of Shamir Yur'ish a century earlier. There is certainly evidence for confusion and disturbance having occurred during the later part of the third century, when there were no fewer than three parties competing for the throne of Sabâ: Shamir Yur'ish, the legitimate holder on the one hand, and the two pretenders, Il-Sharh Yahdib and 'Alhân Nahfân, on the other. The fact that victory ultimately fell to Shamir is not of so much concern to us as are the repercussions which arose from these upheavals. Out of the confusion, it would seem, there emerged a local baron of the Kahlân, as opposed to the Himyar, branch of the Sabaean royal family. This was Rabî'a ibn Mudar, who apparently won a measure of local success besides managing to establish himself as independent ruler of his own stretch of country for at least a while against the consolidating power of Shamir Yur'ish.

There were also strong rumours about an impending Abyssinian incursion into the Yaman, and Rabî'a decided to place at least his family beyond harm's reach. He was encouraged in his plans by a dream that was interpreted by his soothsayers as meaning that the Abyssinians would soon be in occupation. (It might here be relevant to mention Rabî'a's inherited propensity for clairvoyant foresight and seeing disturbing visions, since it was his great-grandfather who dreamed prophetically of the destruction of the Mârib dam and precipitated the stampede of the Arab tribes into the neighbouring desert.)

And so, according to al-Nuwairî (who states it on al-Hamdânî's authority), Rabî'a dispatched his minor son, 'Adî, his womenfolk and all his possessions to al-'Irâq under the care of a nephew called, of all things, Jadhîma. With them he sent a letter of recommendation to the Persian monarch, Shâpûr II Dhû l-Aktâf, whose reign extended from A.D. 310 to 379, and who provided a domicile for Rabî'a's family at al-Hîra. When 'Adî attained to man's estate, Jadhîma married him to his sister Raqqâsh; and it was their son, 'Amrû ibn 'Adî, who succeeded to the throne of al-Hîra after the death of Jadhîma at the hands of al-Zabbâ', who was in turn destroyed by 'Amrû in revenge for his uncle's death. Since Zenobia was most certainly not killed by 'Amrû,

2
Silver dish depicting the Persian king, Shâpûr II 310-79 A.D.

but spent the last years of her life in Italy as a 'guest' to the Emperor Aurelian, the Jadhîma story is clearly apocryphal along its main lines. On the other hand, there is no reason to doubt that he made the migration from the Yaman to al-'Irâq; and the period squares well with the traditional date for the bursting of the Mârib dam, some four hundred years before the birth of Islam.

As the centuries slipped away after the advent of Muhammed, so the mainstream of Islam came at intervals to be swollen, sometimes made tempestuous, by heretical and philosophical tributaries which fed their way in from neighbouring countries, Arab as well as non-Arab. Despite its alternating periods of strength and weakness, of confusion and cohesion, the Baghdad Califate remained a dominant factor in the world as it was known at that time. When Ibn al-Athîr completed his history three years before his death in 1234, the great disaster of the Mongol invasion still lay a quarter of a century in the future. After the transfer of the Califate to the Fatimids of Cairo, and later to the Ottoman sultans of Constantinople, Arabia settled down to a long sleep of six centuries, forgotten or ignored by the rest of civilization.

But Islam continued to flow on in a broad, placid stream of orthodoxy, bordered on the one side by an inscrutable forest of mysticism while on the other it relentlessly flooded the once fertile fields of research and speculation which had inspired the earlier historians. Their successors, warned against trespassing on the forbidden ground of 'higher criticism', needed to content themselves with the springs of fancy and fiction. And, within half a century of Ibn al-Athîr's death, the romances of the *Thousand and One Nights*, inspired by far older tales of Persian origin, had established themselves as the principal element in the literary repertoire of the Arab world.

Despite this it should not be supposed that the more serious historians were altogether put out of business. There was always a market for teachers, and these continued, like their predecessors, to prepare the most elaborate lecture notes and to expand them into their final forms as text books. But the fact remained that the well-springs of their information had run dry, as was only to be expected after six centuries of intensive searching with fine-tooth combs to catch up every scrap of information about the past – however apparently trivial and however impossible to verify – which had survived into Islamic times.

Only one such source had been neglected or ignored by them all, and this was done apparently deliberately. It was nothing less than the deep well into which the early champions and divines of Islam had cast the key of the cupboard which contained the forbidden fruit of knowledge. Their motivation was obvious: to offset all possible chance of contamination of the pure, puritanical doctrines of the new faith by contact with the specious charms of the good old days of paganism, to say nothing of the rival claims of Judaism and Christianity. Even during the nineteenth and twentieth centuries, the Wahhâbîs have seen it as their duty to make short work of any 'subversive' literature which has come within their reach. Even into modern times in Arabia, the study of archaeology has been regarded by certain elements as sinful (*harâm*), while toleration is extended only to the revealed testaments of the Jews and Christians, which are clearly and obviously enough the sources on which Arab historians have themselves so largely drawn.

It was this very narrowness of spirit which placed the tacit taboo on the study of the 'Himyaritic' literature of the ancient Arabs, which remained graven on the rocks and walls. The one fortunate aspect is that there never seems to have been any deliberately organized campaign to eliminate the silent testimony of the stones. But during the long periods when these records were more easily accessible than they are today, Arab historians made no use of them, remaining content to put forward as 'history' a mixture of fact and fable, endorsed by the imprimatur of Islamic orthodoxy. It is only in recent years that the

3
A Sabaean bronze ass with a dedicatory inscription from about 200 A.D.

researches of Western experts have encouraged Arab scholars to enter the field. The light did not really begin to dawn until the middle years of the twentieth century. An indication that it had by then begun to do so comes from an unexpected source: the introduction which a popular and prolific modern writer, Émile Habashî al-Ashqar, wrote to his historical novel, *Bilqîs, Queen of the Yaman* (three volumes Beirût, 1957). In what he has to say he makes the following statement:

> Now you should know that, in all the inscriptions and monuments of the Sabaean epoch which they carried away to Europe, there has been found no trace of the name of the queen Bilqîs, whom some of the historians have sought to place among the kings of the first period: nay, whom they have sought to identify with the 'Queen of Sheba' who visited Solomon in Palestine. But her name has been found [*sic*, since this is unfortunately not the case] among the kings

of the second period, which is the Himyaritic era, beginning in 115 B.C. as I have read. So the Bilqîs, whose story we are writing, was not 'Solomon's Queen'; nay, she knew not Solomon, nor knew he her, nor is there any connection between them. Now Solomon was of the ninth [*sic*] century B.C., while this Bilqîs was of the fourth [*sic*] century A.D. Thus, as you see, there were more than twelve

4
An oryx head, a common Sabaean decorative motif

centuries between him and her. True, the story of Bilqîs, queen of Sheba, and Solomon, occurs in most of the Arab histories; but she was not this Bilqîs, the heroine of our story, nor are we concerned with her. And you will find all that you need to know in the chapters which follow.

Apart from the fact that the name Bilqîs has yet to be discovered in any Sabaean or other known south Arabian inscription, this passage is remarkable in that here an Arab author may be found stating uncompromisingly in print (for the first time, so far as the present author knows) that no connection exists between the Bilqîs of Arabian lore and the queen of Sheba who became immortalized through the visit she made to Solomon. The light is indeed at this point beginning to seep through shuttered windows.

Yet, with the relaxation of the old disciplines which came about as early as the fourteenth century, we might have expected to find at that time an era ushering in a period of more critical self-questioning, at least in lay matters. The puritanical standards of the seventh century must have seemed oddly out of place during the fourteenth, in communities which had become accustomed to wealth and luxury. And to some extent, as the *Thousand and One Nights* makes abundantly clear, there did occur some modifications of moral attitude in the everyday lives of the people. But it was a development which scarcely touched the schools or seats of learning where traditional methods of teaching and study continued to hold sway and went on without interruption. In part this was, of course, because there was no hope of bringing new evidence to bear on already established conclusions; but in part also it was because the professors were themselves eminently satisfied with the validity of the conclusions which had already been formulated.

Like those who had gone before them, the scholars of the fourteenth century saw the authenticity of a story as being dependent on the reliability of the chains of evidence on which it hung. Here and there a tradition might be challenged, or one tradition might be preferred over another, but, by and large, it was always the same, familiar and oft-repeated story which took its place in the history books.

It may today strike us as perplexingly strange that in all the seven centuries which followed the sack of Baghdad and the fall of the dynastic califate, not one single Arab voice was raised to challenge the traditional version of pre-Islamic Arabian history, which thus succeeded in reigning supreme for almost fourteen centuries.

5
A limestone funerary stela depicting a male figure holding a dagger and framed in a border of bulls' heads and rams from Sabâ, first century A.D.

8 *The Legends of Three Ladies*

The historians of the early centuries of Islam were perfectly familiar with the traditions preserved in the Old and New Testaments, as well as with certain aspects of late pre-Islamic Persian and Byzantine history, to say nothing of vague memories of the Achaemenid dynasty and of Alexander the Great, fading into a background of Iranian mythology. They also possessed the tales of Arab chivalry, hande down orally by the poets and minstrels of the century leading up to the birth of Islam; and, above all, the genealogies of tribal Arabia. Beyond these sources, the facts of history tended to begin to become obscured within the mists of fading folk memory. At this point the professional story-tellers took over, gathering up the loose threads of tradition to form a tapestry of legend that came to be accepted as fact by the peoples of the Arab world almost down to our own times.

As we have seen and emphasized throughout the present study, there was only one vital source of information which was studiously and inexcusably ignored, as if it did not exist: the tens of thousands of graffiti and inscriptions which managed to survive the deliberate or accidental iconoclasms of the Arabs and the natural ravages of time. The ruins and rocks of pre-Islamic Arabia are quite literally littered with records of the ancient Arabian kingdoms, listing their rulers and leading personalities, and providing invaluable information on their religious institutions, quarrels, disturbances and warlike activities as well as their economic conditions. With the earliest monumental records dating back to about 460 B.C., they continue from there in an almost unbroken line down to the middle of the sixth century A.D. The total neglect of all this material by the Arab historians of Islam remains especially unforgiveable in the light of the fact that we know from al-Hamdânî and Nashwân ibn Saîd, both natives of the Yaman, that the 'Himyiratic' script was still perfectly easy for them to decipher in their own times.

1
Achaemenian jewellery of the fourth century B.C.

Hamdânî, moreover, does emerge from history as something of a freethinker, an independent intellect who felt impatience at the traditional grooves into which the scholarship of his age seemed to have settled. Towards the end of his days he went to live in the remote north of the Yaman, doubtless in search of the peace and quiet he needed for the completion of his life's work. In the event, he seems to have found the remote intellectual atmosphere of his new domicile somewhat stifling. His reaction to the provincialism in which he found himself was to let off steam by satirizing the local poetasters, who took their revenge by preferring against him the most serious charge of showing disrespect for the Prophet. He was admittedly interested in the study of certain heretical doctrines, and it was probably this preoccupation which in the end earned him the privilege of spending his final days in the prison at Sanâ, where he died in A.D. 945/6.

Living as he did in the Yaman for the greater part of his life, however, amid the Minaean ruins of Jauf and in the Hamdânid plateau, with its numerous recorded evidences of his ancestors, Hamdânî must without doubt have been acquainted with many famous monuments of the past, whose inscriptions he could read without hindrance. Yet, in the few specimens which survive from his work, he unaccountably seems to have failed to appreciate the light which these were capable of throwing on the history of their authors. How wildly astray even

2
Gold staff terminal with lapis lazuli head from Iran, made during the fifth century B.C.

Hamdânî could unconsciously go may be best illustrated by quoting verbatim a passage from his historical writings, told in his own words:

3
Gold hair ornament from the Oxus Treasure fourth century B.C.

> Certain old histories of the Yaman state that, when there was a famine in the world in the time of Joseph (may he be saved), with swarms of locusts, there was distress in the Yaman and the Hijaz and Najd, because the land was so dependent on rain and lacked running water. So Bata' ordered his two sons, 'Alhân and Nahfân, to make application to the treasury of the king of Egypt, who was al-Walîd ibn al-Riyân of the older 'Amâlîq [Amalekites]. Accordingly, they wrote to al-'Azîz in Egypt, who was Joseph (may he be saved), in charge of those who visited him, seeking to trade their merchandise and perfumes, wares and metals. It was he who saw them through all their difficulties and troubles, for many there were whose provisions consisted of locusts. Now, when Joseph saw them, he sympathized with them on the distance of their travels, and mourned their calamities; and he advised them to dig wells, which he described to them. So they returned and dug wells; and all the wells of the Yaman date from that time, being fitted with gear

which requires no cleaning. So they continued irrigating by this means all that time.

Hamdânî gives this naïve and somewhat involved account without comment; and without, moreover, the slightest hint that he is aware of its chronological absurdities. It is only possible to assume that, like his predecessors and contemporaries, he had no conception of the time factor with which he was ostensibly dealing. Joseph's stewardship in Egypt, after all, ended some 1,800 years before the time of 'Alhân and Nahfân.

For the scholars of our own day, the stones of the desert have by now delivered up many of their long-secure secrets and made possible the identification of many of the Abyssinian monarchs who ruled in the Yaman as well as the Sabaean sovereigns who preceded them and then succeeded them during the fourth century of the Christian era. But the stones, as we have said, have continued to maintain their obstinate silence so far as Bilqîs is concerned, whose name does not occur in any authentic inscription. (The only claimant is a bronze or copper plaque which purports to represent images of Solomon and Bilqîs seated at each end of a bench or wall. It was reproduced in Marcel Cohen, *Documents Sudarabiques* (Paris, 1934), but may be safely dismissed as a forgery.)

4
The Temple of 'Athtar at Ma'în, Yemeni Jauf. It is thought that the roof construction of the Temple of Ilmuqah at Mârib may have been very similar

5
Pendant inscribed with the name Wadd, the Minaean moon god

What alternative deductions are therefore left to us from the coverts of legend and genealogy? As has been amply illustrated, we are dealing with a period about which the Arab historians themselves failed entirely to grasp the essentials, but it was a period which played a vital part in the development of both Islam and its institutions. The prevalent paganism of Arabia met head on the challenges posed by Judaism and Christianity, and from the resulting conflict there emerged a new religion, destined to drive out of Arabia the two earlier rival claimants in the field of revealed religion, and also to curb their influence throughout a considerable part of the known world of those days.

As for the preceding centuries of unchallenged paganism, they might be assumed never to have existed if all we had to go on was what the historians of Islam had to tell us about them – despite their strenuous efforts to link events and personalities from relatively more recent times with such historical characters of human antiquity as Nebuchadnezzar and Solomon, Joseph and Abraham, Shem and Noah, even Adam himself. Yet, almost as if in compensation for the gratuitous introduction of the Solomon episode into a story which dates from the third century A.D., the historians ignore the far more vital fact of the Abyssinian occupation of the Yaman which came about during the hundred years which followed.

6
Adam digging in the garden of Eden watched by the Archangel Gabriel, from an oriental manuscript

Where the name Bilqîs does turn up in the genealogies, the identifications for her father tend to vary, but in the end the most likely candidate is the Sabaean monarch, Il-Sharh Yahdib (b. *c.* A.D. 215). This enables us to place the birth of Bilqîs as his youngest daughter at around 250. By any reckoning therefore, Bilqîs would have been a younger contemporary of Zenobia, and a somewhat older one of the princess of Samarqand. It seems that it was the fame and adventures of these three great ladies of the age which fused together to provide the story-tellers with a richness of source material as remarkable as any in the *Thousand and One Nights* or their Persian prototypes. We have, in any case, arrived at the point where Solomon decisively disappears from the scene, though we have no need to doubt for a moment that he was once visited by a queen of Sheba. With Solomon out of the picture, though, we are left with the historical Bilqîs of the Yaman, shorn of the reflected glory of that romantic episode and its sequel, and without any reliable documentation about her life, except for her place in the genealogical tables and the fact of a marriage with Dhû Bata'.

While we can thus pin down her place in history with some precision, we still have no idea who her mother was, once we have safely discounted the story of her semisupernatural origin. We also know that she was never a queen in her own right, or the consort of any reigning king. The imaginary connection with Solomon was merely a nucleus for the story-tellers to work on. They drew their inspiration from more immediate sources, and she certainly lived through exciting times, with wars and rumours of war filling the air in every direction: threats to the Yaman from the north; the Abyssinians conducting their military operations in southern Arabia; and, finally, the Romans bringing pressure to bear on the Arabs of the Syrian borderlands. But there is not an iota of evidence for Bilqîs ever exercising the slightest influence on the course of history, either through action or counsel.

There is, on the other hand, a remarkable resemblance between the stories circulating about her and those which concerned al-Zabbâ' (assumed to be Zenobia) and the princess of Samarqand (though that location was almost certainly never reached by Shamir Yur'ish or any of his successors on the Sabaean throne). One cannot help but suspect that the halo of heroism which attaches to Bilqîs must have been fed in to her story in large measure from the better known and largely historical adventures of Zenobia, though these also have been put through a process of falsification and embellishment by the Arab historians. Nevertheless, it is these stories which seem to provide pro-

7
'The Queen of Sheba's Journey to Solomon' by Piero Della Francesca

totypes for the romances with which the Arab troubadours sought to divert their credulous, sensation-seeking audiences.

These narratives may all be said to be based on three fundamental fallacies, because of the following aspects:

(a) No evidence exists whatsoever for Bilqîs ever having left the Yaman.

(b) The storming of Samarqand by Shamir Yur'ish can only be pure fiction.

(c) The Roman setting of Zenobia's life has been so completely recast in an Arab mould as to create a serious doubt whether al-Zabbâ' was ever intended to be the well-known queen of Palmyra or some other princess of tribal Arabia.

In any case, it was the Zenobia legend which provided the story-tellers with their stock-in-trade: for display in line with the tastes of the markets in which they offered their wares.

Naturally enough, each of these three ladies is represented as possessing certain properties of mind and spirit which might, in the context of their times, be regarded as representing peculiarly masculine preserves, besides showing their own feminine monopoly of exceeding beauty. To deal with the least important and most nebulous member of the trio first, the princess of Samarqand, we may state that she cannot be said to have any particular affinity with Bilqîs. On the other hand, she certainly shared with al-Zabbâ' a feminine passion for jewellery, perfumes and rich materials, as well as the conviction that any would-be suitors should be able to fulfil her desires in that direction. Bilqîs, by contrast, thought it more became her to carry out the wooing herself, sending lavish gifts to the man who might be potential enemy or husband.

The Samarqand lady and al-Zabbâ' both lost their crowns and their lives in puruit of worldly baubles, both falling easy victims to the 'Trojan horse' technique, cunningly manipulated by enemies posing as friend or suitor. But, with the sack of Samarqand, that particular princess passes together with the dissolute king her father beyond the ken of the Arab historians, whose interest in the subsequent military operations of Shamir Yur'ish and his successors in carrying out the subsequent subjugation of Persia and China (Turkestan) inspires a saga of fantasy of desert wanderings. In each case, it is notable that a treacherous minister engineers the king concerned into a disastrous position: in one, the monarch and his entire army perishing of thirst; and, in the other, the father of Bilqîs only being saved by the miraculous intervention of Bilqîs's fairy mother, who then returns for ever to her fairy homeland after delivering the wicked minister to the justice of the sword and producing out of nowhere the little girl whom she had apparently consigned at birth to the mercies of a scavenging bitch.

According to Arab legend, al-Zabbâ', like Bilqîs, succeeded her father to the throne of Palmyra, the latter having been killed in battle by Jadhîma, who was slain by her in turn, she then being warned by her soothsayers of the identity of the man who would avenge this second death by killing her – as, indeed, would happen with the 'Trojan horse' episode in this version. It was a prophesy which fell within the same sequence as the prediction of the Abyssinian conquest of the Yaman which precipitated Jadhîma's emigration to 'Irâq at the time of Bilqîs.

But even more significant links than these exist between the stories of the two ladies with whom we are now dealing. Al-Zabbâ', whose name means 'the hairy one', though it is clearly suggested by the name of Zenobia's father, Zabbai, shared with Bilqîs a reputation for having hairy legs. And each of them exposed her lower limbs to her prospective suitor, with sharply contrasted consequences. Bilqîs did so in response to the trick played on her by Solomon or the devils, Solomon then evidently deciding that she was not a suitable candidate for inclusion in his already immense harem; though he showed sympathy for her disappointment by arranging with the devils for them to invent a depilatory with which to remove her unfortunate blemish without the risks attending the use of a razor.

Al-Zabbâ', however, exposed her legs out of pure malice, to the alarm of an all too trusting lover, whom she then slew without further ceremony, and without letting us in on the secret of what she had revealed to him. In the alternative version of al-Zabbâ''s execution of her suitor, however, he is brought into her presence as a virtual prisoner by the escort which she sent to meet him at their mutual territorial frontier, and is treated with the fullest ceremonial appropriate to a fellow-sovereign. His killing, in this case, is almost a sacred ritual as his veins are opened for the blood to flow. But she has been warned by a witch that, should a single drop of the king's blood be spilt on the common earth, she will pay for her action with her own life; and, indeed, some drops are spilt, despite all the precautions taken to collect the precious liquid in a golden vessel.

Bilqîs, of course, is credited with a similar exploit in her youth, some time before her alleged adventure with Solomon. Her predecessor on the throne was, by some accounts, a king identifiable as the Dhû l-Qarnain of the histories, which state that his tyrannical reign lasted no less than four centuries; though others specify another king, Tubba' al-Aqran (also identifiable with Dhû l-Qarnain), though he, they then say, reigned a mere 163 years; and yet others name al-'Abd Dhû l-Adh'âr, with a positively miniscule reign of twenty-five years. This particular king, at all events, exercised his penchant for deflowering the virgin daughters of the Yamanî nobility, and when he makes his standard proposal (not to be refused) to Bilqîs, she responds by accepting and inviting him to her palace. The wine flows freely at the reception, but the last cup quaffed by the monarch has been doctored with a fatal dose of poison. Alternatively, the meeting of the lecher and the maiden is interrupted by two stalwart young men of the princess's household, whom she has placed in concealment behind the arras of her boudoir; and these emerge at a prearranged signal to cut down the presumptuous ruler with their swords. Thereupon Bilqîs ascends the vacant throne, to reign for 120 years according to some accounts, though for a far shorter period according to others; to be succeeded eventually by Solomon and, after him, his son Rehoboam.

A further point of resemblance between the two stories may be detected in the fact that both Bilqîs and al-Zabbâ' live in palaces that have subterranean tunnels leading away from secret panels in the boudoirs, to provide them with a means of escape in the event of an emergency. Bilqîs, as it happens, never seems to have had occasion to make use of her secret escape route, though the assassins of her predecessor and would-be seducer might well have come through it to obtain discreet access to her boudoir on the night they did their bloody work. In the case of al-Zabbâ', she made the mistake of confiding the secret of her tunnel to a 'friend' who was in fact the ally of her enemy, the person against whom she had been warned by the soothsayer. And, when she used it to escape from the troops disgorged by the 'Trojan horse' trick, she encountered 'Amrû ibn 'Adî barring the exit and eager to avenge his uncle Jadhîma's death. His sword then foiled her attempt to commit suicide by sucking poison from the hollow ring on her finger.

Al-Zabbâ' was presumably buried at Palmyra after she died in this manner, though the historians make no mention of it (and, in any case, we know perfectly well that Zenobia passed her last years as an honoured prisoner-of-war at Tivoli on the Italian coast). It is perhaps no more than coincidence that Bilqîs was also entombed in a secret grave at Palmyra. This was the tomb built for her by Solomon, they said, which was not discovered for many centuries, though when it was the body of the famous queen was found to be intact and in a perfect state of preservation; and was then reinterred in a suitably splendid mausoleum by order of the Umaiyad calif of the time.

The cumulative effect of these resemblances between the careers of three illustrious women of the third century A.D. seems mainly to suggest a common pool of stories, from which the story-teller could select whichever elements chimed in with his own mood or the response of his audience at the time; much like the adventures of Harûn al-Rashîd and the other heroes of the *Thousand and One Nights*. So far as it is possible to separate fact from imagination, it is to the partially verifiable history of Palmyra in the days of Zenobia that we will have to look for any documentary evidence. But the Jewish histories and legends (the Old Testament, the Targums and so forth) do not help us in any way, for they explicitly relate to events and persons far removed in time and space from the Yaman of Bilqîs; though, when they came to be written in their presently known forms, their authors had no reason to believe that the land of Sheba had ever existed anywhere else but where it certainly lay in their own time. It was this conviction which so powerfully influenced the Arab historiographers, who never dared to challenge the authenticity of an outstandingly improbable legend.

The Ethiopian material largely emanated from a fixed conviction of the truth of a popular fallacy, in which there may nevertheless be a grain of truth which has never been brought to light. In February 1960, the last Emperor of Ethiopia, Haile Selassie, during the course of a state visit to Riyadh, was confident and proud in claiming affinity with his royal Sa'ûdî host.on the grounds of his dynasty's descent from the union of Solomon with Bilqîs. Convinced of the all-embracing truth of the legend, he failed to realize that only part of it was dealing with fact.

It may all perhaps best be summed up by saying that the Bilqîs of the Arab legends was, in all essentials, the Zenobia of history, suitably embellished and adapted for presentation on an Arab stage in the august company of King Solomon, the reputed founder of Palmyra. The Bilqîs of history was a very different person: an identifiable princess of the Yaman, the grandmother of Ethiopian kings and perhaps also of the royal line of Sa'ûdî Arabia. The inscriptions of Wâdî Mâsil, not far from Riyadh, indicate that her descendants in the fifth and sixth centuries A.D. were the last Arab kings to rule in Najd until the restoration of an Arab kingdom by 'Abdul-'Azîz ibn Sa'ûd in 1926, fourteen centuries after the disappearance of the Sabaean monarchy under the incoming tide of the Abyssinian conquest of the Yaman.

What therefore has been gained from investigating these odd instances of deliberate self-deception on the part of scores of generations of Arab scholars, who have been accorded, in all seriousness, the rank of competent historians by their fellow-craftsmen the world over? For one thing, it is always worth while to investigate the facts of history and the sources of legend. This may be taken as a common-place of archaeological investigation, which has, during the past two

8
The Great Street of Riyadh

centuries, been responsible for adding so much to man's knowledge of the world in which he finds himself. Some subjects may well be thought to be more worthy of attention than others; but few will deny that one of the most famous romances of antiquity must merit a more serious treatment than has often been accorded to it in the past, either at the hands of the historian, the writer of fiction or the Hollywood scenario artist. Unsuspected items of fact may well emerge from the middens of rubbish that have accumulated over time. It is surprising what may turn up in response to a little scratching at an unpromising surface. It is to that task that the preceding pages have been given over, and in closing we may summarize our conclusions as follows:

First, the queen of Sheba who visited Solomon was not the Bilqîs of Arab history. She may have been the daughter of a king of Edom, or alternatively a king of Midian, named Hadad.

Secondly, the tribe of Sabâ (or Sheba) was in Solomon's time located in northern Arabia, and did not migrate to the Yaman until, at the

9
Riyadh Bazaar

10
'Solomon and the Queen of Sheba' after Sir Edwin Poynter

earliest, the middle of the seventh century B.C., probably under pressure from the kings of Assyria.

Thirdly, the Sabaean monarchy, or empire, was well established in the south by 500 B.C. at the latest, as is attested by its inscriptions which survive from over the following thousand years. Some experts might wish to set this date back two or three centuries, say to 800 B.C., but the palaeographical evidence would be against them.

Fourthly, all these Sabaean kings had quite distinctive dynastic names, as did the Minaean, Qatabanian and other dynasties whom they overran and reduced to subjection. Yet not one of all these names is even mentioned by any of the Arab historians until the middle of the third century A.D. Arab memory in practice extended no further back than about three centuries before the birth of Muhammad, though it professed to remember Methuselah, and even Adam.

Fifthly, the early Sabaeans had no system of dating their records other than that of the mayoral years of their cities (a system which may or may not be based on the Greek model of archonships). But, in the first century A.D., their contacts with Rome led to their adoption of the Julian era, which remained in force until about A.D. 270.

Sixthly, from then onwards, the military exploits of Shamir Yur'ish suggested a comparison with Alexander the Great and resulted in the adoption of an 'Alexandrine' calendar, based on the accession to his throne of Alexander I in 108 B.C. – not Alexander, the son of Philip of Macedon, but the son of Cleopatra, and not *the* Cleopatra at that. This date was obviously defined as the result of a miscalculation by the astronomer-royal of Shamir's court, but the new method of reckoning outlasted the Sabaean régime into the Abyssinian occupation of the sixth century, during which Abraha al-Ashram dated his famous inscription on the Mârib dam in the 658th year of the Sabaean era, or A.D. 550, only twenty years before the birth of Muhammad.

Seventhly, and finally, that the marriages of Abyssinian kings during the fourth century A.D. to Arabian princesses lends strong circumstantial support to the claim of the Ethiopian dynasty and its last representative, Haile Selassie, to have been descended directly from Bilqîs of the land of Sheba, if not from her utterly apocryphal union with King Solomon in a far earlier age.

In the end, however, the rich and complex tapestries of these desert legends and histories could never be expected to surrender up all their secrets. Their hiatuses and contradictions must always remain to tease the minds of those who seek to follow the trails of exploration which they offer; and, when it comes to it, they will live on according to the skill with which the story-teller tells his tale and brings it alive from his listeners' wondering attention.

Select Bibliography

Arabic and other sources for the story of the Queen of Sheba

Di'bil bin 'Alî al-Khuzâ'î: *Dîwân*, ed. 'Abd al-Sâhib 'Umrân al-Dujailî, Beirut, 1972

al-Hamdânî: *Kitâb al-Iklîl*, i-ii, ed. M. bin 'A. al-Akwa', Cairo, 1963-66

al-Iklīl (al-juz' al-thāmin) by al-Hasan ibn-Ahmad al-Hamdāni, ed. N. A. Faris, Princeton, 1940 (translated by N. A. Faris, *The antiquities of South Arabia, being a translation of the eighth book of al-Hamdāni's al-Iklīl*, Princeton, 1938)

al-Iklîl, x, ed. Muhibb al-dîn al-Khatâb, Cairo, 1367 A.H.*

Nashwân bin Sa'îd al-Himyarî: *Die himjarische Kasideh*, ed. and tr. A. von Kremer, Leipzig, 1865

Mulûk Himyar wa-aqyâl al-Yaman, ed. A. I. al-Mu'ayyid and I. bin A. al-Jarâfî, Cairo, 1378 A.H.

Ibn al-Athîr: *Ibn-el-Athiri Chronicon quod perfectissimum inscribitur*, ed. C.J. Tornberg, 14 vols., Leiden, 1851-76

Ibn Ishâq: see al-Tabarî, *Annales*

Ibn al-Kalbî: see al-Tabarî, *Annales*

Ibn Miskawaih: *Tajârib al-umam*, ed. L. Caetani, 3 vols., London, 1909-17

Hamza al-Isfahânî: *Hamzae Ispahanensis annalium libri X*, ed. and tr. I.M.E. Gottwaldt, 2 vols., Leipzig, 1844-48

'Abîd bin Sharya al-Jurhumî: see 'Abd al-Malik ibn Hishâm, *Kitâb al-tîjân fî mulûk Himyar*, Hyderabad, 1347 A.H.

D. D. Luckenbill: *Ancient Records of Assyria and Babylonia*, 2 vols., Chicago, 1926-27

al-Mas'ûdî: *Maçoudi, les prairies d'or*, ed. and tr., C. Barbier de Meynard and Pavet de Courteille, 9 vols., Paris, 1861-77

Akhbâr al-zamân, ed. 'Abdullâh Ismâ'îl al-Sâwî, Cairo, 1938

Makhtasar al-'ajâ'ib, ed. B. Carra de Vaux, *Les abreges de merveilles*, Paris, 1898

al-Nuwairî *Nihâyat al-'arab fî funûn al-adab*, 18 vols., Cairo, 1923

J.B. Pritchard (ed.): *Ancient Near Eastern Texts Relating to the Old Testament*, third edition, Princeton, 1974

al-Tabarî: *Annales quos scripsit Abu Djafar Mohammed ibn Djarir at-Tabari*, ed. M.J. de Goeje *et al.*, 15 vols., Leiden, 1879-1901

**anno Hegirae*, in the year of Hegira – i.e. from the flight of Muhammad (A.D. 622)

al-Tha'labî: *Qisas al-anbiyâ'*, ed. A.A. Saiyidal-Ahl, Singapore, 1382 A.H.

al-Wâqidî: *Kitâb al-maghâzî li-l-Wâqidî*, ed. Marsden Jones, 3 vols., London, 1966 (partial translation in J. Wellhausen, *Muhammed in Medina, das ist Vakidi's Kitab al-maghazi, in verkurzter deutscher Wiedergabe*, Berlin, 1882

al-Ya'qûbî: *Ibn Wādhih, qui dicitur al-Ja'qubī, Historiae*, ed. M. Th. Houtsma, Leiden, 1883

On the Queen of Sheba generally see most recently J.B. Pritchard (ed.), *Solomon and Sheba*, London, 1974

Index

Index